VIRTUALLY
LOST

Essays on Education in a
Global Pandemic

ANDRÉ BENITO MOUNTAIN

FOREWORD BY BARUTI KAFELE

Includes Essays By:

MARCHELL BOSTON
JONIE HARRIS
JUAWN JACKSON
ERIN JONES
JEFF MATHER
E.B. MCCALL
WILLIAM MUSTAFA
IANTHA USSIN

Interior/Exterior Graphic Design by André Benito Mountain

Cover Images by William Mustafa, Jr.

Virtually Lost/André Benito Mountain. –1st ed.
ISBN 979-8-712-098903

Also by André Benito Mountain | Principals
Don't Walk on Water | The Brilliance Beneath |
The Mountain Principles

"It's not the note you play that's the wrong note – it's the note you play afterwards that makes it right or wrong."

— **Miles Davis**

Dedication

This book is dedicated to the memory of
Dr. Patrick Calvin Pritchard.   As a professor at
Wesleyan College, he mentored hundreds of
teachers into this profession. His work and ideas
continue to transform schools and classrooms.

Table of Contents

ACKNOWLEDGEMENTS

In 2020, I published Principals Don't Walk on Water: They Walk Through It. That book shed light on the experiences of an early career principal, encountering and overcoming the struggles of leading an urban school in a community undergoing significant demographic changes. The book opened up the doors for me to have dialogue with many other educators about their experiences leading and teaching in schools. What I learned from that experience was that while our titles and career paths may diverge, our shared desire to effect social change through our work with children is a common bond.

This book would not have been possible without the many conversations I've been able to have with committed educators from nearly every corner of this nation. We have celebrated one another, traded war stories, and tried to encourage one another through an unbelievable test of our collective fortitude. I would like to thank the Jeremy Anderson Group for your support and encouragement. Your work with schools and with those who want to add value to schools is immeasurable.

I would also like to thank the contributors to this book for your transparency and your commitment to sharing your story in a time when educators need to know they are not in this struggle alone. Many thanks to my former 5th grade student, Mr. Juawn Jackson on your appointment to the Bibb County Board of Education. My first job as a teacher was with Bibb County and you were one of my students. To see you now as a member of the board and as a contributor to this book is a full circle moment. Thank you for continuing to dream. Thank you to Dr. Marc Boston, a true superhero in the DeKalb community. The Fantastic Freedom Middle School is lucky to have you as their leader. Jonie Harris, you are a gem. Continue to shine brightly in the city of Tacoma. Our children need more teachers like you. Thank you, Mrs. Erin Jones, for remaining as a beacon of light for educators. Thank you, Ms. Iantha Ussin, for your authenticity and for coming through with your insight! Thank you, Mr. William Mustafa, for capturing the image that would become the cover of this project. I appreciate your expertise and artistic guidance. Thank you, E.B. McCall, for managing to balance motherhood, teaching, and writing. You embody what many teachers must accomplish on a daily basis. Thank you to the teachers at Belmont Runyon Elementary School. I can't wait to come visit you all very soon! Many years ago, as a classroom teacher, I was able to work with site artist Jeff Mather. I complained the entire time because I wanted to close the door of my classroom and just teach Reading and Social Studies. Jeff and a wise principal, Bequi Coar, taught me that the school experience becomes more meaningful when we get students outside of the classroom and engage them in creative projects. You've joined the Marbut Traditional Theme School community and have been doing amazing work with our scholars on Engineering Design. Thank you for your contribution to them and to this project.

Thank you to my loving wife for your listening ear and wise counsel as this book was written. Thank you, Tierney, for teaching me what virtual learning looks like from a student's perspective. Thanks to you, I have gotten a better idea of how this experience has affected students.

Thank you to the schools and universities who have contacted me to engage your students and staff about the work of educators. I appreciate your support and the space you provide for me to inspire and engage in dialogue about transcending the spaces that have limited public education for decades.

Thanks to the platforms that regularly share my writings: Education Post, Citizen Ed, BrightBeam, Education Week, Principal Magazine, Teach Magazine, and Washington Principal Magazine.

The many successes shared in this book would not be possible without the assistance of my leadership team: Ms. Lyseight, Ms. Arrington, Ms. Tanks, Ms. Dennis, and Ms. Blakely. To the Marbut Traditional Theme School team, may we all continue to live out our school motto: Commit to the Challenge. Let's continue to create spaces where children thrive.

Finally, I want to thank Baruti Kafele for contributing his time and voice to this project. As an aspiring school leader, I drew inspiration from your videos and writings. I reached out to you and BAM! You came through for me. I am honored to have you as a contributor to this project and as a brother in the struggle. Your leadership is shaping the profession in a tremendous way.

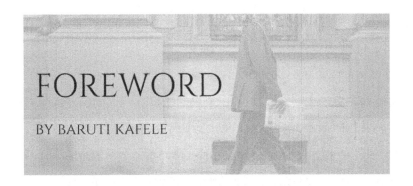

FOREWORD

BY BARUTI KAFELE

As I type, it is the month of March 2021 - the one-year anniversary of the closure of schools in response to the spread of COVID 19 across the U.S. Looking back, February, 2020 was a typical month of schooling in America. I recall vividly the work I was doing as a consultant throughout the month of February in America's schools. And then all of a sudden, one month later, the world shifted, and we found ourselves in the midst of a global pandemic. Schools were immediately closed and education as we knew it came to a screeching halt. There was panic in the air - "How will the children be educated? What will this mean for historically oppressed and marginalized students, particularly Black and Brown students? In addition to a health crisis, we are in an education crisis which could have generational implications!" Panic was truly in the air.

As a temporary solution, schooling across the country and abroad became virtual. In addition to the reality of not being afforded a "dress rehearsal" before "opening night," many teachers had to be trained in using the various virtual platforms immediately. In other words, in order to provide young people with a semblance of what they were accustomed to, teachers had to be trained on a new pedagogy…overnight. Moreover, as we converted to virtual instruction and learning, the inequities became magnified. Many, and I mean many in Black and Brown communities had no computers in their homes and / or no internet access. The only way to educate them was through work packets while districts and state departments of education scrambled to get these children computers and internet access. It was also discovered that many teachers who live in remote rural locations had no internet access themselves and had to drive long distances to areas where they could get internet access such as coffee shops and parking lots. And then of course, the impact on parents economically was immeasurable, not to mention the toll that COVID 19 took on the health and the lives of hundreds of thousands of people across the country, including myself.

And now, one year later in 2021, here we are....trying to recover, trying to reopen schools, trying to rid ourselves of this virus but it's an ongoing challenge. Are there any positives; silver-linings; lessons or findings we can build upon? Absolutely. I want to share one here – Parental Engagement. Traditionally, in many schools, particularly urban and rural schools beginning at the middle school level, it can be a challenge to engage parents. Specifically, it can be a challenge to get parents to come out to schools for various meetings, workshops, trainings, programs and parent – teacher / parent – administrator conferences. Although it is easy to look at a parent's lack of engagement at the school level and conclude that "he / she doesn't care," when examined through an equity lens, this is typically a grossly inaccurate conclusion. There are in fact a plethora of justifiable reasons that a parent may not be able to attend a school function that must always be considered. Our reaction to the pandemic relative to the use of virtual platforms has provided a viable answer.

Considering the volume of laptops that we discovered that districts and states could actually afford to provide families, inclusive of hotspots and other forms of internet access for economically disadvantaged families, there is not as great of a need to have parents attend their children's schools for the aforementioned reasons. Instead, these communications can all occur virtually which will increase the volume of engagement both exponentially and immeasurably. I have been saying for the past year that if I were ever to return to my principalship, I would create a culture with the parents where an evening once weekly principal – parent mass meeting virtually would be our norm in an effort to keep parents informed, engaged, inspired and empowered. This would be a win for the entire school community.

Yes, the pandemic has created an endless number of challenges which has rendered us "Virtually Lost," but it has also provided us with new opportunities which we must seize upon as we move forward. You will find many of those opportunities in this great and necessary book.

Baruti K. Kafele
March 2021

André Benito Mountain

INTRODUCTION

"Throughout history, it has been the inaction of those who could have acted, the indifference of those who should have known better, the silence of the voice of justice when it mattered most, that has made it possible for evil to triumph".

Haile Selassie, Emperor of Ethiopia
— Cited as from an address in Addis Ababa (1963)

The 2020-2021 school year was one that reminded all educators what if feels like to be lost at sea. Waves crashing all around us, crew members looking for land in the distance. As the ship tilts and tumbles, people are very clear on what they need to do to shift the sails and keep the vessel afloat. This is a book about overcoming in that moment when all seems lost.

Many of us have missed the sights and sounds of school. We have longed for the rich community that classrooms filled with children provides for us. Our children have missed being in class with their peers and engaging in the socialization that school provides. We all worry about how much school closures will impact the progress of our most at-risk students.

This time has also taught me lessons about being more intentional as I seek input from teachers. In many instances, we have dropped the ball on making sure we listen to the people who are tasked with caring for our scholars.

When everything that was once familiar is virtually lost, all we have to return to is our reason for doing this work. That is what will sustain us. As you read the writings of educators, artists, and principals in this book, please know and understand that this is just a snapshot of the range of emotions that we all experienced during one of the most transformative moments in the history of American education.

My hope for this book is that it can be a guide for school leadership teams as we all begin the healing process of bringing our school communities back together. There will be no return to 'normalcy' because the space we were in previously did not serve all of our children well. My hope is that we come back better, stronger, and more responsive to the needs of the families we serve. This means we expect more technology for homes in communities that are traditionally underserved. We demand wrap around services for families who are struggling with issues of poverty and trauma. We need rich and meaningful after-school programs and stronger community partnerships to better support the work of schools.

This book includes checklists for schools to use as they think through the concepts outlined in the chapters. There are questions that should be posed and discussed with members of the school leadership team that can guide the work of schools as we look to improve in ways that are not always measured by traditional metrics. I want to thank my dynamic leadership team for your undying support and guidance as we have steered the ship through turbulent waters.

While we may have felt the uncertainty of being virtually lost as some point during school closures, being lost is not synonymous with being hopeless. We are still filled with the hope that education can uplift our young people to reach their potential. Our schools, like our country, have drifted off course. But with an army of talented and committed educators standing in the gap, we have the potential to get on course. Being lost means that we are paying more attention to what we are seeing, looking for landmarks, patterns, and adding to what we already knew with a broad array of new findings, software, approaches, and strategies. Being virtually lost does not denote hopelessness or defeat. It simply means we may need to stop someone and ask them to point us in the right direction. This collection of essays intends to do just that.

André Benito Mountain

Atlanta, Georgia

March 24, 2021

Chapter 1: Grand Opening, Grand Closing

By André Benito Mountain
Principal

"If by their fruits we shall know them,
they must first grow the fruits."
— Kwame Nkrumah,

This was going to be our year of redemption. But to truly understand the space that we find ourselves in right now, I have to take you back a few years. I want you to understand why this year meant so much to us, and how we are coping with the disappointment of not being able to provide our scholars with the full Marbut experience. Our story is the archetypal hero's journey. The global pandemic and school closures were just additional challenges we faced along the way to us fulfilling our destiny as a cornerstone of our community.

During my first year at Marbut Traditional Theme School, we saw incremental gains in student achievement, and we celebrated it with vigor. We met as a team and tried to determine what were the areas where we demonstrated strength and what changes we could make as a collective to continue to move in the right direction. Did we have the right systems in place? Were people working in their areas of strength?

Our legacy as a school was one of high-expectations and an emphasis on structure and self-discipline. People relished in the fond memories of what we once were, all the while losing sight of the changing context of public education where growth, progress, and social-emotional supports needed to be the focal points of our efforts. The times had changed since our founding in 1996 and the community and the complexities of life for the students we served was demanding that we too develop new perspectives and approaches to reach our goal of increasing the effectiveness of our school. We were providing food to families dealing with issues of domestic violence. We were providing school uniforms to scholars who were outgrowing theirs. We were conducting morning meetings to help create spaces where children could be heard and valued by their peers. We'd been recognized by the school district for increasing our PTA membership.

When the 2018-2019 scores arrived, we were disappointed we had not met our goal. It would be more accurate to say that we were devastated. But champions don't make excuses, they make adjustments. This was what needed to take place at every level of our school. We eventually were able to look deeply into our current state and began strategizing a way forward. That's part of the reason this book is so significant. Not only does it place the pandemic in the context of the story of a school that is on its own quest to improve, but it also shares the experience of having a moment of victory virtually lost in the process. As principal, I needed to remind people that we were more than scores on one test taken on one day in May. We were an idea grounded in high levels of parent engagement, teacher accountability, and academic excellence. We could not let one year of disappointing results change how we saw ourselves. So, we picked ourselves up, and began to reimagine what we represented.

"The South Got Something to Say…"

My advice to anyone who is winning at this moment is to never forget how people treat you when you are not winning. Those folks who stand with you in the most difficult moments are the ones you should pull into your inner circle. Some colleagues who used to call or connect with me at meetings stopped calling and connecting. It was a humbling experience that taught me lessons about my own fortitude and sense of resolve to turn things around.

I began to feel what I imagine Andre 3000 felt when he walked on the stage at the 1995 Source Awards after winning Best New Rap Group:

> *"But it's like this though, I'm tired of them closed minded folks, it's like we gotta demo tape but*

don't nobody want to hear it. But it's like this.. the South got something to say, that's all I got to say."

-Andre 3000

The one year of not having met our performance targets became our scarlet letter. It was as if we had never had any other data points. It became the central topic of every conversation about our school. What we didn't realize at the time was that due to the upcoming cancellation of subsequent administrations of the Georgia Milestones, we would be stuck with this score for years to come, never having an opportunity to emerge from under the cloud of doubt.

Turning it around would have to be a team effort. It would require my entire leadership team to be more vested in the work we are doing. I would tell them, "Your silence doesn't serve the team. If you have an idea, please put it on the table now so we can have the benefit of your insight." New systems would need to be developed and new measures implemented so we could monitor our progress along the way and adjust as needed.

Since that time, we've seen tremendous success as a as a school. Our scholars have exceeded growth projections in Reading and Mathematics on Classworks diagnostics. Most grade levels are experiencing their most significant increases in RIT scores in years on the NWEA MAP assessments. Our staff has provided feedback on the Insight Survey, administered by TNTP, noting improvements in family engagement, peer culture, and professional development well above the national average. Parents are responding positively on surveys about our school-wide communication and supports for their scholars.

How did we pull it off during a global pandemic?

We rebuilt our systems and took a long hard look at ourselves. We'd been writing and discussing our continuous school improvement plan, but we weren't monitoring it at the levels we needed to in order to see the results we expected. This was the most pivotal adjustment we made during the 2019-2020 school year. We created a culture that valued honesty and lifted up the voices of every member of the team. When there were tough calls to be made, I'd gather the input of my leadership team and teacher leaders to get a better sense of how the issue was seen by others. We monitored our progress along the way, holding ourselves accountable for keeping one another focused. Meetings aren't conducted without agendas. Most importantly, meetings are not held unless they are absolutely necessary. I value and honor the time of members of my team. As a leader, my responsibility is to demonstrate that respect of their time by not keeping them waiting on me to arrive at a meeting or conducting excessively long meetings when they have other personal and professional commitments. Teams understand what our expected outcomes are for their collaborative planning structures. Book studies are held and everyone on the team is expected to participate and grow from the experience. Every meeting begins with celebrations of our incremental progress. If no one else is going to celebrate our efforts, we must find the value and joy in what we are doing for our scholars and for this community.

That's why this book includes some of the questions we posed during our meetings to guide our thinking. These are the questions that other school leaders and leadership teams might find useful as they look to reexamine their own processes and procedures. While we still have challenges to overcome as we gradually reopen our doors, we are in a much better place now than we were at the onset of the Covid-19 pandemic. We've become more strategic about our weekly and daily routines. I've introduced my administrative team to Michael Hyatt's Full Focus planning method, setting priorities for each quarter, week, and day. I see elements of this approach in their work, and it also becomes part of the culture of our school.

Discussions during collaborative planning are more data driven than before. Teachers are in the driver's seat, sharing their screens virtually and talking through usage data on programs like iReady and Classworks. They are conversant in achievement data, and actively sharing ideas with colleagues on how to improve the instruction of specific grade level standards.

Let us begin to change the culture of our profession by resisting this tendency to immediately devalue people, schools, and communities as they undergo the ups and downs of improving student achievement in urban spaces. A bit more empathy is needed to understand the circumstances that make the work of educators and school leaders increasingly complex. Let us continue to probe and offer support, knowing that each school and community is facing its own sets of challenges. Even as teachers were working from home during the pandemic, there were comments being made about the effectiveness of instruction being done from home. It was as though members of the general public did not believe that professionals could deliver solid instruction without being housed in the school buildings. We've proven that we can deliver under the direst of circumstances. We were committed to the challenge and determined to stand in the gap for our families who were depending on us.

This was to be our first year with a set of triplets in our school. Having had a few conversations with the parents over the summer, I knew that the parents shared my excitement of having them join a unique school that they'd heard great things about. We had it mapped precisely well in advance. The siblings would be placed in three different Kindergarten classes. What an amazing adventure they would have entering our school together and growing into their own unique sense of identity over the years of being enrolled in our school. The triplets did enroll and join our school community this Fall, but their experience has not been anything like we'd imagined due to a virus that has not only changed the experience of one family, but reshaped an entire profession, forcing us to evolve and adapt. The words of Maya Angelou saying, "Stand up straight and realize who you are, that you tower over your circumstances" could not be more fitting than in this moment for our community of scholars and educators who have had to stand up. It's in those moments of difficulty that leaders are forged, and the impurities are burned off in the process.

Shadows of Black Trauma

The Covid-19 pandemic has emerged in the shadows of unprecedented Black trauma. The crime rate in metro-Atlanta has reached a peak in recent months. Nationally, we've seen more deaths of Black people at the hands of law enforcement. Many educational professionals are starting to feel the psychological effects if isolation, quarantine fatigue, and the added stress of having to redesign their instructional delivery in a mostly trial and error fashion this year. What is the cost of silence for educational leaders? So many of us who lead schools remain silent in the midst of it all. One of my teachers recently asked me, "Don't you worry that 'they' will monitor what you write and say something about it?". Educators in urban communities have a responsibility to shatter the silence in the service of social justice. Thankfully, I've positioned myself in a district that doesn't shy away from issues of social justice. From launching a district-wide Black Lives Matter initiative to supporting the My Brother's Keeper initiative, they understand who we serve and the time in which we live. The families served by schools in my community were already wrestling with the ravages of unemployment, broken homes, and poverty. Grandparents were raising the second generation of children as their own. School districts were aware, but not yet responsive to the urgency of creating 1:1 schools where every child had a device. The delay in scholars getting devices issued by school districts has helped some families reflect on those Black Friday big screen television purchases when children need access to instructional technology beyond the school day. How are our priorities, districts, and households, impacting our children? All of us, especially communities of color, were trying to live in an America under assault of the Trump presidency. As he intentionally scraped the wounds of race and civility, our communities were the first to bleed at the hands of armed police officers. Each thoughtless tweet was another blow at an already teetering level of civility. The pandemic presented us with questions that we would have to grapple with over several months:

- Which communities will be most impacted by the school closures?
- How will the digital divide be addressed by an incoming administration in Washington?
- What autonomy will teachers have to make decisions about school reopening?
- How will we confront the role of high-stakes testing and how we evaluate schools and teachers in the post-Covid reality?

But more than anything else, the pandemic let us see ourselves for what we'd truly become: A society so suspicious of our institutions that we at first saw it all as a hoax, then with the data in hand, refused to believe the professionals. Now, with the highest death tolls in the world, we continue to flirt with the idea of sending our educators and children back into schools where they are at risk of contracting a life-threatening virus. At this moment, we all pray that our district-level leaders are as intent on data driven decision making as they are when we analyze student achievement for sub-groups in our schools.

Lost Traditions

"I think she can go the rest of the way on her own", I whisper in passing as a subtle suggestion to well-intentioned parents who want to walk their child to class day after day each Fall. One of the joys of the principalship is seeing Pre-Kindergarten and Kindergarten parents walk into our school holding the hands of their timid four or five-year-olds. The mission they are embarking on is one of momentous significance. Photos are taken. Tears are shed. On occasion, parents watch and wave as a scholar insists on walking to class on their own on this first day in a remarkable show of independence. Sadly, we haven't experienced this rite of passage since the Fall of 2019. Instead, we've welcomed them into virtual classrooms where children exist in a virtual community where they can only see their classmates on the screen. It's an awkward arrangement where teachers can glimpse into the homes and lives of their students and get a feel of how they live and the environments from which they come.

Another tradition in our school that brings back vivid memories of joy and community is our Honors Day, held at the end of each semester. It's a time when we celebrate the efforts of our scholars. Along with my assistant principal, I stood on a stage and shook the hands of hundreds of scholars for several hours. Covid-19 had made an indelible mark on us as a school. If we return to the format of the large assembly programs in the future, we will likely replace the handshake with another gesture to celebrate them.

There's still a bit of a philosophical rift about honors and awards lingering in the air. As much as we want every scholar to be honored, we insist that scholars earn what they receive based on rigorous grade level standards. Gone are the days when everyone in the class receives something just for showing up and sitting in a desk. Let's send a message to our scholars early in their educational careers that the world owes you nothing. What happens when you consistently give children awards and accolades they have not earned? They come to expect it. We want our scholars to understand that their scholarship and academic progress rests upon the blood, sweat and tears of centuries of people who were denied education and fair treatment. Many of them overcame tremendous obstacles to learn to read or earn a portion of the education that is afforded to our scholars. They must understand this.

Sense of Belonging

This year, one of my goals was to go deeper in creating a sense of belonging in our school community. While we might not be together in the building, I wanted to make sure there was no doubt about who we were and what our legacy was. Founded in 1996, our school is a true partnership between parents and teachers to set higher expectations for scholars. Our school song, which speaks to that idea of doing what others say can't be done, became a central part of the weekly announcements. One of my parents was a recording artist, so he offered to rerecord the song for us with an updated vocal arrangement. It reminded us all of the scene from "Lean on Me" when Principal Joe Clark marched those young men to the music teacher's class and said "I certainly never authorized you to change it...Mrs. Powers, you've rewritten our alma mater". The song became the anthem for a rebirth of Eastside High. I don't remember my elementary school having a school song, but I want to engrain the lyrics of ours in the minds of our scholars this year more than ever.

After a few weeks of virtual learning, I realized that having all of my scholars arrive in their virtual classrooms wearing their school uniform shirts was another step in the right direction. We continued to emphasize the importance of morning meetings as a way to forge a sense of classroom community. Our school design includes the requirement that students complete projects each semester. Despite calls from some parents and one staff member to eliminate the projects this year, we decided that this part of our school design would not be compromised since we were not in the building. Leaders have to determine how they will respond to the forces that are acting upon their respective schools. What will be the cost of the school closures? What experiences will we adapt to the new reality and which ones will be set aside until later? How can we as school leaders continue to help our schools evolve despite school closures? Here's what we knew for certain. Students were still capable of conducting research and presenting their projects virtually. Parents were still available to support scholars in choosing a topic. Projects could be presented virtually by scholars sharing a screen or uploading a completed presentation in a number of alternate formats. Volumes of books exist on how to deliver engaging lessons, build on prior knowledge or enhance rigor. Those are the easy parts of our profession. No one has written the handbook on how to open a school while it remains closed. There's much work to be done to script the way to bring an entire school community with rich and deep roots of celebration collaboration together via virtual platforms.

Reevaluating Our Relationship

The global pandemic has forced us to confront how we view schools. Every relationship reaches a point when we have to determine why we are in it and what our expectations are. We've discovered that some families view the school/home relationship as primarily a childcare and supervision arrangement while they are either at work or home. Other families have continued to view the school as a vehicle for their children gaining access to college and careers. Among the ranks of our educators, we've been able to see who our most committed educators are in the midst of this remote learning environment. We've also been able to determine which educators struggle with self-management, technology, and deep commitment to the mission of the profession. The depth, quality, or lack of plans only brings heightened visibility to a teacher's performance, broadcasting the level of preparation and expertise into households. For my scholars and families, this is the only teacher they will know this year. Let's not compromise on the quality of our profession at its most critical hour. This is our grand opening during our grand closing. The decisions we make at this moment will determine the texture of our impact for years to come. Whether we work together or use this moment as a time to turn against one another, we will have children standing in the wake of our decision-making.

Our profession is improvising much like Miles Davis in the "Ascenseur pour l'Echafaud" video where he is looking up at the screen and creating the notes to match the moments in the film. We are reaching into the depths of who we are to capture the moment in all its beauty, opportunity, and tragedy. It is inherently flawed, raw, unrehearsed, and unscripted.

CHECKLIST:
BUILDING OPERATIONS

☐ HAS MY DISTRICT ENHANCED THE VENTILATION IN ALL CLASSROOMS? HOW DO I KNOW?

☐ HAVE ALL TEACHERS BEEN PROVIDED WITH ADEQUATE PPE TO PROTECT THEMSELVES AS THEY TEACH IN A HYBRID SETTING?

☐ HAS THE SCHOOL LEADERSHIP ESTABLISHED A PROTOCOL FOR ALL BUILDING OPERATIONS (CUSTODIANS) MEMBERS TO CLEAN AND SANITIZE FREQUENTLY TOUCHED AREAS IN CLASSROOMS AND AROUND OUR SCHOOL?

☐ DOES THE SCHOOL LEADERSHIP HAVE A DAILY OPERATIONS WALK OF THE BUILDING TO IDENTIFY AREAS OF CONCERN?

☐ HAS A SYSTEM BEEN ESTABLISHED TO SAFELY DISTRIBUTE LUNCHES TO CLASSROOMS TO MINIMIZE MOVEMENT IN THE SCHOOL?

☐ HAS A TEAM OR COALITION OF COMMUNITY MEMBERS BEEN ESTABLISHED TO HELP SUSTAIN THE APPEARANCE OF THE EXTERIOR OF THE CAMPUS (GARDENS, LAWN).

☐ HAS A SIGN-IN SYSTEM BEEN ESTABLISHED TO SAFELY MONITOR ARRIVAL TIMES WITHOUT HAVING FACULTY AND STAFF CONGREGATE IN LARGE GROUPS?

☐ DOES EACH MEMBER OF THE SCHOOL OPERATIONS TEAM HAVE A CHECKLIST OF THE TASKS THAT MUST BE COMPLETED IN THEIR ASSIGNED AREAS BEFORE THE END OF EACH DAY?

Chapter 2: Pandemic Line Leaders

By Dr. Marchell Boston
Principal

Feelings of exhaustion, frustration, confusion, and uncertainty have become the norm during lengthy district principal meetings during the pandemic. These 2–3-hour virtual huddles include school district leaders, the superintendent, senior-level cabinet members, principals, department heads, and various central office departments. These meetings which were once held monthly have evolved into bi-monthly sessions. The district focus areas and highlights are reiterated during district regional principal meetings. Common themes in both meetings include the expectation that all staff must report to the building to prepare for students. While it has been stated that all staff must report, it has also been stated that we should do our best to lead with compassion and provide flexibility with staff as it relates to reporting to campus to receive students. Another common theme is that principals must ensure that their respective buildings are ready to receive students.

These common themes have resulted in principal work sessions/support sessions after district and or regional principal meetings. The sessions involve brainstorming on ways to meet expectations for staff returning to the building, while simultaneously leading with compassion. Additionally, principals have brainstormed and shared ideas about specific action steps to ensure that their buildings are ready to receive students. The pandemic has resulted in higher levels of collaboration among school leaders as we all seek action steps to best lead our schools. We have been forced to extend our critical friends to include colleagues in various parts of the district, as well as colleagues in other districts. Many principals like myself, have sought suggestions from colleagues via social media.

John Maxwell contends that "if you think you are leading, but no one is following you, then you are only taking a walk." Maxwell's quote speaks to the influence of leaders. It beckons leaders to examine the degree of followership of the individuals that they lead. The question for leaders is, "Are people following my lead? or "Are people carrying out my vision?

Strong leadership is more important today than ever before. The Covid 19 deadly virus has impacted our world, our communities, and schools in an unprecedented fashion. Government leaders are at odds about whether schools should open or remain closed. Additionally, there are various schools of thought regarding safety precaution measures. Some states and districts are requiring facial masks, while other states are not requiring masks. The dissenting opinions among decision-makers regarding school safety and health has added additional stress and responsibility to school-based leaders.

I, like many of my colleagues, take pride in making the best decisions for the students and staff. Leading during a pandemic brings about thoughts of prerequisite courses or experiences that have prepared my colleagues and I for today's challenges. The reality is that are no prerequisites for the leading a school during a pandemic. School leaders were involuntarily enrolled in the Leading during a Pandemic class in March 2020. The content and information presented during my Leading during a Pandemic class has been guided by CDC as well as our respective districts' Covid- 19 Task Force. Throughout the class, I have also reflected on indicators of effective leadership during a pandemic.

The class line leader is responsible for taking a safe route to a destination in a school. Similarly, school leaders are responsible for making decisions that result in our students and staff being safe spaces. I surmise that many of today's school leaders served as line leaders as students. My line leader experiences were very gratifying. As a line leader, I was the first student that everyone saw as my class walked down the hall. The line leader job made me feel proud. I knew that I had done something well to get the job. I also knew that my peers my covenant job. Most importantly, I was in control of the line and everyone was following me.

The juxtaposition of emotions of being the line leader and the pandemic leader can be linked to lack of prerequisites and changes in the position of the CDC. As a one-time confident line leader, who was sure that I was leading my class to a safe place in the school, there have been times when I have questioned if I am leading my school to safe spaces. The initial meetings that were part of my Leading during a Pandemic class focused on plans for students to return once the Covid -19 cases lowered. In December 2020, the meetings focus shifted based on CDC guidance. The meeting emphasis then and now is opening schools and reducing the likelihood of spread by employing mitigating strategies to include universal and correct use of masks, social distancing, hand washing, cleaning, and contact tracing.

As a once confident line leader, I am not confident about schools reopening for face-to-face instruction. As Covid-19 related deaths continue to increase, I wonder if decision-makers value economy over humanity. I acknowledge the fact that some of my students are in dire need of face-to-face instruction from their teachers. I am also concerned about the mental health and physical health of staff members who have expressed their anxieties during countless one on one meetings. These concerns have often been expressed in the form of questions: How can the school ensure that I won't get Covid? What if a student gets Covid, what happens next? Am I am being forced to work, although I have a pre-existing health condition? What are my options as a caretaker of my elderly relatives? Will I lose my job if I don't come to work?

Leading a school during a pandemic has made me stronger believer and leader. There have been times in which I have questioned my influence and wondered if was leading or if I was simply taking a walk. After reflecting on the last nine months, I am convinced that I am indeed providing effective leadership in a pandemic. While I don't completely endorse the reopening of schools, I am able to highlight school related positive outcomes of the pandemic. Staff capacity increases in instructional technology use is the most significant positive outcome. Additionally, the staff has explored and implemented various ways to communicate and build relationships with stakeholders. Lastly, the pandemic has strengthened an already strong family bond among the staff. We are stronger, we are better, so much better. We are beating the odds amid a pandemic together. The 2019-2021 school years will always be remembered as the years of the pandemic. My experiences of leading a school during a pandemic have been an invaluable part of the journey. It has taught its own lessons about what leadership and life have to offer.

CHECKLIST:
LEADERSHIP STRUCTURES

☐ DOES MY LEADERSHIP TEAM HAVE A STANDARD MEETING TIME WITH STRUCTURED AGENDAS?

☐ DOES EVERY MEMBER OF OUR SCHOOL LEADERSHIP TEAM HAVE A DESIGNATED AREA OF RESPONSIBILITY WHICH THEY MUST DISCUSS DURING THE LEADERSHIP TEAM MEETING?

☐ HAS OUR SCHOOL ESTABLISHED PLATFORMS FOR PARENTS TO SHARE THEIR CONCERNS VIA COMMITTEES OR IN INFORMAL SETTINGS?

☐ HAS OUR SCHOOL ESTABLISHED STRUCTURES FOR STUDENTS TO VOICE THEIR IDEAS AND SUGGESTIONS TO THE SCHOOL LEADERSHIP TEAM?

☐ DO MEMBERS OF THE ADMINISTRATION PROVIDE STAFF AND PARENTS WITH SURVEYS TO GAIN FEEDBACK ON THEIR CONCERNS AND QUESTIONS?

☐ DURING PARENT MEETINGS AND SCHOOL EVENTS, DOES THE ADMINISTRATION SHARE DATA FROM SURVEYS WITH THE SCHOOL COMMUNITY?

☐ HAVE PARENTS BEEN PROVIDED WITH WAYS TO OFFER THEIR SERVICE TO THE SCHOOL IN THE FORM OF VOLUNTEER HOURS OR DONATIONS TO SUPPORT THE SCHOOL?

☐ HAS THE SCHOOL ADMINISTRATION SET UP A STRUCTURE FOR TEACHER LEADERS TO BE ABLE TO SHARE IDEAS WITH THEIR PEERS WITHIN THE SCHOOL?

André Benito Mountain

Chapter 3: Seven Tips for Principals to Move the Needle Now

By André Benito Mountain Principal

"Hip is to know, it's a form of intelligence. To be hip is to be update and relevant. Hop is a form of movement, you can't just observe a hop, you gotta hop up and do it. Hip and hop is more than music Hip is the Knowledge, hop is the Movement. Hip and Hop is Intelligent movement."

-KRS-ONE

Leadership has always been about being reflective, innovative, and pushing people out of their comfort zones. There are multiple needles to move to create a school that is vibrant, connected, and equitable for a diverse community in metro-Atlanta. What do our scholars and communities deserve? They deserve schools that are vibrant in the sense that everyone adds something to the school beyond their typical role. The vision has to be salient and pervasive. Making that idea of vibrancy and collective effort clear to everyone requires some creativity and persistence. While some members of a team naturally devote themselves to the overall mission, others require more compelling illustrations of how they fit into the legacy we are crafting. My leadership style samples the ancient pedagogical use of analogies, used by Plato, Socrates and Jesus in teaching concepts and developing understanding in groups. Plato's Allegory of the Cave is a perfect example of using symbols and scenarios to illustrate a deeper meaning. Dr. Martin Luther King, Jr. used a powerful analogy to describe America when he said, "I fear I am integrating my people into a burning house." When asked what we should do, he went on to say, "Become the firemen. Let us not stand by and watch the house burn." It was an analogy that conveyed a reflective and honest assessment of what he saw and what needed to be done.

Months after school closings and stay at home orders were issued by some cities, something interesting happened. D-Nice stood at two turntables and helped us, if only for a moment, forget that the world as we knew it was crumbling. D-Nice not only played music for us to lift our spirits, he reminded us to live, to dance, to vote, and to give to worthy causes. We watched him groove to the music himself, clapping and singing along as he led the gathering he dubbed Club Quarantine. With traveling limited and many live venues closed, he found a way to continue his work in a different format, much like what our schools have been called to do in this moment. He listened to requests posted in the chat, gave shout outs to listeners, and created a sense of community among people who had never met before his hands touched the turntables. He brought millions of people into his home to share an experience that exemplifies what great school leaders must do to move needles now.

Work-life balance has been an ongoing conversation with my staff this year. With students and staff isolated from one another for almost a year, we all have had to adjust from an analog experience to digital platforms for schooling. Learning to unplug from our work and tap into our passions has become a call to action that even principals must embrace as we lead teams virtually. I began to think of how D-Nice's arrival in this space emerged out of a crisis. His normal venues were closed, and he sensed a need to bring music to the people during a time of heightened anxiety about the pandemic. It was innovation at the most organic level. Identify a need and develop a solution that steps beyond the limits of what we've done in the past. It's the challenge that I present to my staff and leadership team each day.

D-Nice ignited a movement by leaning into his passions. What are the leadership lessons school principals can 'sample' or 'remix' into their own crate of strategies? What are some essentials for moving needles now on student achievement and school culture? Principals, aspiring principals, and those who currently support principals should know these 7 techniques principals need to move needles at this moment in public education.

M.A.R.A.U.D.S.
1. **M**onitor the Chat
2. **A**djust the Levels
3. **R**ecognize the Team
4. **A**cknowledge the B-Side
5. **U**nseal the Vinyl
6. **D**ig in the Crates
7. **S**ample

The unpredictability of D-Nice's changes in hats reminded me of the rhythm of our work as educational leaders. School leaders have always worn many hats and adjusted their movements to the beat of many different drums. There is a growing collection of hats principals must wear to manage virtual and hybrid schools such as the distribution of devices, monitoring of virtual classrooms, and orchestrating ongoing professional development. In Hip-Hop culture, the dj was once the central figure, often promoted as the headliner. The names of groups would start with the dj followed by the emcees. There was Grandmaster Flash and the Furious 5, DJ Jazzy Jeff and the Fresh Prince and Eric B and Rakim. Eventually, dj's began to play a different role in the culture as emcees and lyricism took center stage. Even in our schools, leaders have to know when to pause and endure painful silence, troubleshoot a technical issue and when to push others to the front of the stage.

Even in our schools, leaders have to know when to pause and endure painful silence, troubleshoot a technical issue, and when to push others to the front of the stage.

#**1**
MONITOR
THE CHAT

As D-Nice pushed the crossfader back and forth, transitioning to a new track, we posted comments in the chat. We watched the numbers of viewers as they reached the millions. We subconsciously collected data and talked about it with friends. News broadcasts did features on "Club Quarantine". Each week, we hoped to see him top the previous week's numbers, so we called and texted one another when he went live. His success was a collective win. Every school leader working during this time of virtual learning and beyond needs a comprehensive measure of success for teachers, students, and school culture. At least three times each year, teachers and parents should complete a survey that assesses whether the needle is moving as it should. Everything needs to be measured. Operations, professional development, collaborative planning, and leadership all need data points.

Monitoring the chat means listening with a discerning ear. Is it an idea, suggestion, or gripe? Is the idea student-centered or intended to make life easier for adults at the cost of students? During his Club Quarantine sessions, D-Nice monitored the chat, laughed at some of the suggestions, honored others, and thanked viewers for their input. Creating a culture where people feel free to share is a never-ending challenge as you are leading a team. State requirements and national mandates sometimes leave little room tor teacher input. District directives with short timelines for implementation add another layer of urgency that can minimize the voice of teachers on some school decisions. Aside from these moments, the leader can open up the line to 'take requests and suggestions' from the team. It adds texture to the culture of the school. Change is as instrumental to the ever-evolving culture of schools as turntables are to Hip-Hop.

Change is as instrumental to the ever-evolving culture of schools as turntables are to Hip-Hop.

#2
ADJUST
THE
LEVELS

Have we drifted from our initial priorities we laid out during pre-planning? Are we still focused on our school improvement goals? Are educators and parents getting the supports they need? Leaders need teachers on their staff who are courageous enough to be completely honest about the school's trajectory. Every school will have areas of strength and opportunities for growth. The hope is that those taking the survey approach it with a sense of our collective self-efficacy. It's incumbent upon leaders to follow-up and share the data with the staff, leading them through a conversation that may become somewhat tense. Like D-Nice, leaders are adjusting the levels, mixing tracks, monitoring the chat and responding to requests. If parents want more communication, we must oblige them. If teachers want more feedback, we must oblige them.

It's what I call "Instructional Inertia" where an individual or organization resists any and all forces that attempt to move them beyond their current state.

A teacher once said, "But we've always done it this way!" It's a notoriously confining statement that can derail positive change in any organization. It's a normal tendency to try to replicate past successes. It's what I call "Instructional Inertia" where an individual or organization resists any and all forces that attempt to move them beyond their current state. The topography of the school community is not smooth but scratched with grooves from years of stops and starts, new policies and priority shifts. Moving the needle can be a battle. Monitoring the levels of growth and program implementation means overcoming the fear of change. We find a routine and become married to it like sheet music, insisting that notes be played a certain way every time. We find ourselves stuck like a needle caught in a groove on an old 45-inch, wailing the same blues of pain and regret. Principals need the courage to lift the needle, clean it off, and place it in a different spot when things aren't moving forward. Staffing changes and schedule changes can be extremely uncomfortable for some. When the music changes, it takes everyone a moment to figure out what just happened.

Sometimes instead of an abrupt change, a gradual fade is a much better approach.

When the music changes, it takes everyone a moment to figure out what just happened. Sometimes instead of an abrupt change, a gradual fade is a much better approach.

#3
RECOGNIZE
THE TEAM

The turntabalist sets the mood of the room as much with his selection of vinyl as with his enthusiastic commentary. He looks through the chat or into the audience and shouts out people by name. He recognized members of the team who helped make everything possible. "I see you!" Everyone loves to be acknowledged for their efforts. Some prefer it publicly and others appreciate a simple note of thanks. Honoring effort and innovation creates a foundation for everything else.

Moreover, principals must be reminded that each member of the team has something to contribute to moving the needle. Tapping into that broader circle of talent is the secret ingredient of the most successful organizations. Tedious tasks given to school leaders with short timelines require delegating portions of the work to those who can offer expertise and who aspire to one day move needles in their own roles as leaders. An academic coach, a grade chairperson, or a gifted teacher all have ideas and experiences to contribute to co-produce our next professional development. No one is allowed to only show up for the party once all of the equipment has been unloaded and set up. Everyone has something to contribute behind the scenes to help us move the needle once the mics are on.

#4
ACKNOWLEDGE
THE B-SIDE

When albums were pressed, record labels would generally put the song that was intended to get more radio play on the A-side. The B-side was reserved for songs that were less popular in the mainstream. Songs on the B-side of the album sometimes included instrumentals. Feedback is the A-side of our work of moving the needle because it is easy to gather from parents and teacher. A leader's responsiveness is the B-side to feedback where their actions are more instrumental. It is the less popular, less comfortable part of moving the needle.

In other words, the B-side of leadership is becoming more self-reflective. Understanding that the role of the school leader is not exclusively centered around effecting change in students and managing others. Leaders who become fixated on this portion of the role can quickly destroy the soul of a school. Death by micromanagement isn't a research-based practice. At their core, great leaders emerge out of an understanding that they must examine and reexamine their own practices. This B-side of the leadership experience is less popular and often overlooked by aspiring leaders. Baruti Kafele's Virtual AP Leadership Academy was and continues to be a source of deep professional insight for my role as a school leader. He emphasizes the questions a leader must ask oneself as they enter this role.

#5
UNSEAL
THE VINYL

In my collection, I have a sealed Sugar Hill Gang record. It's a rerelease of Rapper's Delight, the first Hip-Hop single to reach Billboard's Top 40 in 1980. Sealed records are great for collectors, but for a vinyl enthusiast, the skies open when the needle touches the vinyl. Schools and districts can unknowingly become collectors of programs and resources that remain sealed, unused or underutilized by those who need them. Leaders need clear and consistent processes to monitor usage of programs and software. Each expenditure is an investment intended to move the needle. Before we can honestly say "It wasn't effective", we must first ask ourselves whether we used it with fidelity and whether the usage was monitored consistently.

Virtuosity in any creative or academic pursuit is rare. Unsealing the vinyl means not only using program, products and resources in our classrooms. It means opening up the books and literature that sheds light on what we want to accomplish in our school. Books like "I Choose to Stay" by **Salome Thomas-El** helped shape the vision of what I wanted to accomplish as a school leader. Years later, I was leading a school of my own and teaching urban youth the game of chess to help them develop better decision-making skills.

#6
DIG IN THE
CRATES

The real test of leadership is whether you have the knowledge and skill of developing leadership in those around you? If the people on your leadership team or staff aren't consistently tasked with trying out new skills, sharing with others, and adding to the strength of the team, the school never reaches its full potential. School leaders need professional development that prepares them to be both analog and digital at once. They need to be analog in the sense of being able to 'read the room', pick up on the feedback, and make adjustments at the right moment. Some songs aren't meant to be played in their entirety. A dj knows when to fade, when to repeat a chorus, and when to make a hard shift into a completely new track.

Ask any leader "What have you been reading lately?" and you will learn much about who they are and what they will become. Yes, our work is time-consuming and maintaining a work-life balance is a skill. Carving out time to search for new ideas and innovative approaches to solve problems is akin to a dj *digging in the crates* looking for those rare, dusty samples that can be adapted into something au courant. Every leader should take an honest self-assessment of how they spend their time, including time spent watching sports and movies. Then, compare **that** amount of time with the amount of time we spend reading and studying to improve our practice as leaders. What gets scheduled gets done. Research on moving the needle on student achievement and improving school culture is abundant. Time is finite.

Carving out time to search for new ideas and innovative approaches to solve problems is akin to a dj *digging in the crates* looking for those rare, dusty samples that can be adapted into something au courant.

#*7*
SAMPLE

Once the leader has spent time 'digging in the crates' researching innovations for moving the needle in a specific area, a decision must be made. Which practices fit for my school community? Which pieces of new information can help move us forward without overwhelming the existing improvement strategies? After Hip-Hop began to move away from using disco tracks, DJ's and producers began using technology to sample a portion of a record, creating a loop that could become the foundation for something unique. What was once the Isley Brothers' **"Between the Sheets"** transforms into Notorious B.I.G's **"Big Poppa"**. MF DOOM reincarnates Anita Baker's **"Been So Long"** into **"Zatar"**. The Genius of MF DOOM is two-fold, simultaneously giving new life to his writings under a new moniker and bringing his selected samples to a new generation of listeners.

Looking through my school re-entry plan or continuous school improvement plan, you'll find elements borrowed from the plans of schools from around the country. The format for many of the extra-curricular activities we offer to our scholars is *sampled* from successful programs that have already been implemented with the positive outcomes we aspire to see. We extract the portion we need, slow it down, speed it up, add a few other elements to it, and let it play for a few months.

Finding your footing as a school leader means continuing to lean into your gift with **gravitas**, using these 7 techniques in proportions that fit the goals you've laid out. Next, you have to determine if it works for the team you've assembled. There is no standard formula, but rather similar ingredients in various proportions. I will allow the greatest lyricist of our time, Rakim, who once wisely reminded us to **"Follow the Leader"**, to have the last word regarding techniques:

They never grow old techniques become antiques.
Better than something brand new 'cause it's original.
In a while, style'll have much more value.
Classical too intelligent to be radical,
Masterful, never irrelevant mathematical.
Here's some soothing souvenirs for all the years
They fought and sought, the thoughts and ideas.

It's cool when you freak to the beat,
But don't sweat the technique.

CHECKLIST:
MOVING THE NEEDLE

☐ **MONITOR THE CHAT:** ARE THERE ONGOING OPPORTUNITIES FOR SCHOOL LEADERSHIP TO HEAR AND ADDRESS CONCERNS FROM FACULTY AND STAFF?

☐ **ADJUST THE LEVELS:** HAS THE SCHOOL LEADERSHIP TEAM ANALYZED DATA AND DETERMINED AREAS WHERE CHANGES NEED TO BE MADE TO IMPROVE STUDENT PERFORMANCE?

☐ **RECOGNIZE THE TEAM:** DOES THE CULTURE OF OUR SCHOOL PLACE A PRIORITY ON CELEBRATING THE ACCOMPLISHMENTS OF TEACHERS AND GRADE LEVEL TEAMS OR DEPARTMENTS?

☐ **ACKNOWLEDGE THE B-SIDE:** DOES OUR SCHOOL ENCOURAGE EDUCATORS TO BE REFLECTIVE PRACTITIONERS? DO TEACHERS HAVE OPPORTUNITIES TO VIEW THEIR TEACHING VIA VIDEO OR AUDIO RECORDINGS AND REFLECT ON HOW TO IMPROVE?

☐ **UNSEAL THE VINYL:** HAVE WE COMPILED A LIST OF ALL OF THE PROGRAMS AND SOFTWARE WE HAVE PURCHASED? IS THERE A SYSTEM ESTABLISHED TO MONITOR USAGE? IS USAGE POSITIVELY IMPACTING STUDENT ACHIEVEMENT?

☐ **DIG IN THE CRATES:** IS THERE A WELL-ESTABLISHED PROFESSIONAL LEARNING COMMUNITY IN YOUR SCHOOL? DO MEMBERS OF THE FACULTY AND STAFF EMBRACE A CULTURE OF ONGOING, JOB-EMBEDDED PROFESSIONAL LEARNING AS A PATH TO SCHOOL IMPROVEMENT?

☐ **SAMPLE:** DOES MY SCHOOL CREATE PROCESSES FOR TEACHERS TO OBSERVE ONE ANOTHER'S EFFECTIVE TEACHING PRACTICES, DISCUSS TEACHING MOVES AND IMPLEMENTATION?

Chapter 4: A Newspaper During the Pandemic

By William Mustafa Jr.
Artist

I ,William Mustafa, am an artist, and one of the tools I use to create my artistry is a camera. With so many people in the world with a camera at their disposal at any given time, I have a chosen to express myself through the genre of documentary photography.

A genre in which one captures images of real situations, candid moments to tell a story or express a particular narrative as it occurs in real time without posing or interfering in the moment in any way.

In one of the hundreds of times Ive ventured into the cities across the world, my most recent outings have been filled with much creative anxiety. The world has changed recently and as of February 2020, the country Ive currently been residing in (Milan, Italy), has been horribly impacted by the Corona Virus COVID19. Unlike other nations across the globe, Italy has been quick to react to the rising numbers of deaths and after China, my particular region was struck with a wave of death, rising fast and crashing down quickly on our society resulting in flood of governmental restrictions.

As citizens we were commanded not to leave our homes while mandatory work from home orders were put in place to prevent the spread along with nationwide closure of all businesses that were nonessential. Federal and local penalties were soon to follow by all municipalities with prison sentences given out to any who were caught trying to wade in the waters, illegally leaving their county of residence not to mention being caught outside for any other reason other than exercising 200 meters from their personal domicile.

This new way of life as an individual who captures the lives of others in the "streets" consequently put a serious damper on how I tell the stories of the "everyday people" in their natural habitat.

This restriction of movement continued for 7 long months and without notice the Prime minister eager to keep up national spirits called for families to come to their windows and balconies, while keeping to social interaction restrictions – gave instructions to speak to each other and see the neighbors who were usually shadows like the trees outside our windows on a sunny day.

Interesting how people you never knew now become so important when all you have are the walls that surround you from day to day. As the numbers decreased the announcement was made in late July that we would be able to venture back out into society with caveats that we keep our required distance and mask our faces to shield from any unwanted asymptomatic disease spread.

Armed with my camera I awaited that morning like Christmas to young children, my camera bag filled with unnecessary gear akin to a full plate at a buffet for one who has not had a solid meal in some time.

Trying to get comfortable in my occupation, each shutter press became more comfortable as I took steps deeper into the depths of the city.

My hearing tuned in to tire sounds, bird chirps, and muffled conversations of people that passed me on the sidewalk. I observed how individuals interacted, how people no longer greeted each other in the traditional way with kisses to each cheek. Where warm embraces used to be, 6ft waves and elbow touches filled the space of the 500-year-old manners of giving salutations.

I tried to take in with my lens the way I was at a loss of understanding by the acute personal feelings that are normally expressed through the smiles and gestures held in faces of people I hadn't met. Each gesture is a clue to a person's personality and there always seems to be a story in every movement. Being a documentary photographer teaches you something on every outing that presents rewards to my passion with a continuous education.

After about an hour out, an older gentleman caught my eye as he walked smoothly through the crowd.

Adorned in a well-tailored suit, sunglasses and vintage Tom Ford shoes, the sounds of his wingtips echoed off the marbled streets like the performing tap dancers in Harlem. Finally, amongst the faceless crowds this stranger started to "speak" to me. I took chase following in his prestigious footsteps, trying to stay anonymous while creating compositions that spoke to the moment him and I were having together. The longer I followed, the more conversations we created. I noticed more and more things about this unnamed man now showing his age through his weathered skin that whispered tales of at least 7 decades.

His slow gate expressed that he was in no hurry to return home, but his steady stroll in a particular direction had an intentional directive. I increased the speed at which I was traversing the sidewalk avoiding multiple trees and pedestrians that came in between my subject and I. Garnering enough space between us, I kneeled on the ground awaiting him to pass in front of my camera framing the classic Italian architecture in the background, positioning a small Iron fence in the foreground hoping he would pass at a moment without any person posing obstacles that would distract from the visual narrative him and I had started 3 city blocks ago.

I needed to understand the point of our impromptu meeting, documentary photography requires a clear narrative.

What lesson had he taught me in our exchanges? In our final interaction his "frame" crossed my frame in singular solitude. Through my camera's viewfinder time stands still when the snap of the camera shutter takes the place of any ambient sound the city produces. I can see everything in this half inch squared cubicle. The imprint of a wedding ring and the days newspaper held in the grip of blue latex covered hands.

A man who I never met but shared the same interest in what was going on in society after a long hard 7 month stretch of seclusion from the rest of the world.

After all my "ins and outs "of the civic crowds and keeping myself at a substantial distance from strangers, not to protect myself from the unseen threat, but to keep my images candid. This pandemic has created barriers between us as humans through masked faces and arm length conversations along with strange glances at the sound of any sudden sniffles.

Though in retrospect it has broken down the walls for me to not only see the world through the minor gestures we tend to mime unknown to ourselves. It also has made me much more sensitive to the apparent "tells" that express the inner emotions of the feelings of a passerby. Covid19 has left us much more sensitive to ourselves and the world, but in closing I was always taught to make the best out of every situation and to always come out a more educated individual regardless of what life tosses at us.

My camera and digital stills are not just snapshots of moments that have past, but a reminder of a way of the life we used to have prior to COVID19 and has put much more emphasis on how I capture imagery going forward.

Who knows what's yet to come, but I will ensure we have a beautiful record of what is.

CHECKLIST: DOCUMENTING THE SCHOOL EXPERIENCE

- [ ] HAS A STAFF MEMBER BEEN DESIGNATED TO COLLECT IMAGES AND VIDEOS DOCUMENTING THE EXPERIENCES OF THE SCHOOL DURING THE SCHOOL YEAR?

- [ ] HAS A SHARED FOLDER BEEN CREATED TO ALLOW MEMBERS OF THE STAFF TO UPLOAD IMAGES CAPTURED DURING THE SCHOOL YEAR?

- [ ] ARE ALL ISSUES OF THE SCHOOL NEWSLETTER UPLOADED TO THE SCHOOL WEBSITE FOR EASY ACCESS BY THE SCHOOL COMMUNITY?

- [ ] ARE SCHOLARS ENCOURAGED TO SHARE THEIR EXPERIENCES IN WRITING OR VIDEOS?

- [ ] ARE THERE OPPORTUNITIES FOR PARENTS TO SPEAK ABOUT THEIR EXPERIENCES WITH VIRTUAL LEARNING ON VIDEO OR IN PRINT?

- [ ] HAS A TEAM OF TEACHERS AND PARENTS BEEN ASSEMBLED TO HELP DEVELOP A YEARBOOK TO DOCUMENT THIS YEAR?

- [ ] ARE THERE MEMBERS OF THE STAFF DESIGNATED AS ADMINS ON THE SCHOOL'S SOCIAL MEDIA AND WEBSITE TO REGULARLY MAKE POSTS AND UPDATE THE PAGES WITH CURRENT EVENTS?

André Benito Mountain

Chapter 5: Reglas Para Los Negros

By André Benito Mountain Principal

"That until the philosophy which holds one race superior and another inferior is finally and permanently discredited and abandoned; That until there are no longer first-class and second-class citizens of any nation; That until the color of a man's skin is of no more significance than the color of his eyes; That until the basic human rights are equally guaranteed to all without regard to race; That until that day, the dream of lasting peace and world citizenship and the rule of international morality will remain but a fleeting illusion, to be pursued but never attained".

Haile Selassie, Emperor of Ethiopia

The shifts and pivots we'd been forced to make along the way were innumerable. Remaining positive through it all meant finding solace in the fact that we were doing everything we could do to continue to provide a highly structured and academically challenging environment for our scholars. Beyond the state approved standards, there is a level of education scholars need that only certain schools and certain teachers can provide. Some school districts fear venturing down the road of social justice for fear of offending some members of their community. The atrocities we've witnessed over the last decade against African-Americans in America provide strong jolt of reality for educators. The recent shootings in Atlanta at Asian spas brings additional attention to the climate in American where hate crimes are on the rise. How will we prepare our scholars to live in this society? Most importantly, how will we prepare them to transform it? What work have we done with our faculty and staff to unpack and address issues of bias?

Just along Euclid Avenue, tucked away between a smoke shop and an African market, in one of Atlanta's most eclectic neighborhoods is a Mexican restaurant that doubles as one of my favorite locations for writing on weekends. I order the ceviche, a traditional Peruvian dish of seafood, lime, and avocados. I think briefly about Ms. Lecaro, an elderly Ecuadorian woman in Union City, New Jersey who first introduced me to the dish in a third-floor apartment along Kennedy Boulevard. Ceviche is made by blending shrimp and crab together with onions, avocado and drenching the mixture in fresh lime juice. The acidity of the citric juices reconfigures the proteins in the seafood, 'cooking' them while they marinate. In a thick Ecuadorian accent, she struggled to explain to me how to make the dish myself, which I only attempted once. As I settled in for an authentically South American experience, I'd instead experience the American South in all its fullness.

A sign has been taped to the front door of El Bandido Mexican Restaurant that reads "Mask Required". As I pull the handle, the door squeaks like an old saloon door causing a few people to turn their heads. I smile underneath my pale blue surgical mask because ever since the mask requirement has been implemented in metro-Atlanta, I feel that I enjoy a level of anonymity as I move through the city. I'm not recognized by anyone now. No longer am I forced to make an abrupt exit from a store or restaurant when I see a problematic parent or scholar who I'm not in the mood to encounter. I'm a masked literary crusader moving discreetly through the city unbothered as I "write the wrongs" of the Black American experience. Anonymity has its limits though. Certain features aren't hidden by the masks we wear and certain infections are more insidious and deeply rooted than Covid-19.As I approach the stand, I'm greeted by a familiar face.

"Amigo! Just one?", he asks. Angel is a middle-aged Latino man. I'm not certain where he is from, but I've noticed in previous visits that he effortlessly vacillates between English and Spanish, sometimes in mid-sentence. He is affable and tries to remember my orders, making me feel like a familiar patron when I'm there.

I nod. "Just one."

"Inside or outside?"

I think for a moment about it and opt to sit outside given all of the commotion inside the restaurant. Between the music and the chatter from the customers, I wouldn't be able to settle into my thoughts and get much writing done.

"I'll sit outside today".

He pauses and says, "Ok, well we will need to hold your ID if you sit outside. We've had a few people leave without paying."

I declined that proposition, knowing how forgetful I am about leaving my ID at a place. I'd take my chances sitting inside today at one of the high-top tables. El Bandido represents many things to me. It represents my support of a minority-owned small business. Using my dollar to support our solidarity and self-determination as minorities in America is a point of pride for me.

He nods and leads me to a table about six feet from the entrance. I unpacked my bag and began to delve into my writing. When the ceviche arrived, I took a break from my writing. Less focused on the words on the page, I could now see that the restaurant had become even more packed inside.

The door opened with that familiar screech and in walked three white females. As they were greeted, I could see them looking around the restaurant. Seating was limited. Their only option would likely be outdoor seating. I began to wonder if Angel would ask for all three IDs or just one from the party. I wanted to see how Angel would slide it in so that it landed well. How would they respond once he shared the news that an ID had to be surrendered to sit outside?

He asks, "Just three today?". They all nod as they look around the restaurant.

"Inside or outside?"

They look at one another and one of them whispers through her mask, "Outside." He reaches underneath the podium, grabs three menus, three bundles of silverware, and whispers, "Follow me."

There was no mention of "leaving IDs" or of "people leaving without paying". Angel was gleeful, seating them in a corner of the patio where the sun cast bright rays of warmth upon the three of them. They removed their masks and got comfortable as Angel chatted with them about the specials of the day.

The food was South American, but the experience was one characteristic of the legacy of the American South.

Here in Little Five Points, on a tree-lined street in the mecca for Black Americans, I was experiencing the microaggressions that compelled James Baldwin to characterize our country as the "yet to be United States of America". The food was South American, but the experience was one characteristic of the legacy of the American South. This brief encounter was layered with prejudice, White privilege, and inter-minority microaggressions that speak to assumptions about the character of people of color.

My grandparents grew up in communities where the need for them to work caused many of them to leave school by the third or fourth grade. At polls, African Americans were given literacy tests in states like Georgia, Alabama, and Mississippi. The generation of African-Americans born around the 1920s would have experienced this widespread effort to disenfranchise them using literacy as a technicality. Because of that, I take my role as a school principal very seriously because I am only the second generation in my family to finish high school and attain a college education. But this wasn't 1924 and this wasn't a dusty coffee shop at a rural train depot. This was in the heart of the Black Metropolis. My mind is racing now. I'm thinking about the relationship between Latinos and African-Americans. I'm thinking of the Jim Crow laws of the South that designated certain areas in establishments for people of color. I'm dismayed that my effort to support a minority-owned business was tainted by what appeared to be a blatant injustice.

"Nah, Angel wouldn't do me like that would he?", I thought to myself. I kept looking back at the patio door, waiting for him to return from taking their drink orders after he seated them on the patio. As the door of the restaurant opened again, rays of light hit the wall and my attention shifted to the large picture of a Mexican bandit and the name of the restaurant, El Bandido. Roughly translated as "the outlaw" or "the bandit", I felt like I'd just been robbed. Those three minutes seemed like an eternity, then the door opened. With his three menus in hand, Angel was headed in my direction. Since my mind had been racing, I hadn't yet had a chance to get my words together, but I knew that I was going to stop him and say something. There's a saying among writers that you don't find books, but rather books find you. I am a writer, but at this moment, I hadn't yet found the words, but I was certain that when he approached, the words would find me.

I navigate through Little Five Points because it is one of the destinations in Metro Atlanta where I feel creatively free amongst the artists selling their portraits on the street and the musicians performing on crowded sidewalks. This incident was an affront to all that the area represented to me.

"Maybe I'm reading too much into this" I thought for a moment. Then I reminded myself that the fight for freedom is not only won in those moments that are highly visible and monumental. Real freedom and change have to reach down into the city, stroll down Euclid Avenue, and touch the soul of people like Angel who perpetuate discriminatory practices in their day-to-day existence. These small assaults on our dignity as men and women of color grow into Briana Taylor incidents, Armaud Aubury incidents, and George Floyd incidents. A police raid at the wrong address, a jog through a neighborhood, or a traffic stop should not be the precursors to Black death. Left unchecked, we die a bit every day when we continue to internalize the American reality.

I beckon for Angel to come by my table. He rushes over and I pull my mask down and say, "Hay reglas para los negros?" He pauses, touches his head as he recalls my initial request to sit on the patio and his response. Stunned by my statement and the lexicon in which it was delivered, he walks away.

I'll miss the ceviche.

This experience taught me that there is still much work to be done in the area of raising awareness of lingering issues of social justice, White privilege, and implicit bias in the communities we serve as educators. At times, it is people of color whose work as educators may exacerbate achievement gaps unknowingly by lowering their expectations for students from disadvantaged backgrounds.

Our willingness to share our own experiences with this ugly and painful part of the American experience is essential in helping to eliminate it from our society. In this instance, it was a restaurant experience, but in other instances that I won't discuss here, it is the treatment of African American people in the criminal justice system. Do members of our school communities understand the power of their own collective voices? Do they know how to galvanize support around meaningful causes and leverage their solidarity to effect change? If not, these are areas where schools and school leaders can step in to point them in the right direction. It could mean writing letters to have a school zone light fixed, or attending a school board meeting to express concern over an issue that will impact their neighborhood school. Without the knowledge of how to use our collective voices effectively, many opportunities to effect change will be virtually lost.

CHECKLIST:
SOCIAL JUSTICE

☐ DOES OUR SCHOOL ACTIVELY EMBRACE A VARIETY OF PERSONAL EXPERIENCES, VALUES, AND WORLDVIEWS AS PART OF THE CULTURE OF OUR SCHOOL? IF SO, WHAT IS THE EVIDENCE OF THIS?

☐ DO SCHOOL LEADERS DEMONSTRATE A REFLECTIVE MODEL OF LEADERSHIP THAT ENCOURAGES OPENNESS, COLLABORATION, AND INFORMATION SHARING?

☐ DO TEACHERS IN OUR SCHOOL HELP STUDENTS TO ENGAGE IN ONGOING DISCOURSE AND ESTABLISH A CULTURE THAT IS COMFORTABLE WITH DISSENT?

☐ DO SCHOOL LEADERS IN OUR SCHOOL HELP TEACHERS TO EXAMINE GAPS IN THE CURRICULUM WHERE MORE CULTURALLY RESPONSIVE CONTENT CAN BE SHARED IN ADDITION TO THE REQUIRED STATE STANDARDS?

☐ DOES OUR SCHOOL DEVELOP FLYERS AND SIGNAGE AVAILABLE IN OTHER LANGUAGES REPRESENTED IN OUR SCHOOL COMMUNITY? IF NOT, WHAT SUPPORTS ARE NEEDED TO ACCOMPLISH THIS?

☐ DO TEACHERS IN OUR SCHOOL FEEL COMFORTABLE HELPING STUDENTS TO CONSTANTLY QUESTION THE WORLD AROUND THEM, INCLUDING THE SCHOOLS THEY ATTEND?

☐ DO MEMBERS OF OUR FACULTY TRULY UNDERSTAND WHAT SOCIAL JUSTICE EDUCATION ENTAILS? DOES MY SCHOOL ADMINISTRATION LEAD DISCUSSIONS ABOUT THE IMPORTANCE OF SOCIAL JUSTICE EDUCATION IN FACULTY MEETINGS, PROFESSIONAL DEVELOPMENT, OR IN GRADE-LEVEL MEETINGS?

André Benito Mountain

Chapter 6: Will All Hope Be Lost?

By Iantha Ussin
Educator

One of the greatest things I fear is letting down my people. I wouldn't live with that type of conscience, of having let down my people after they've been brutalized for so long.
-Winnie Madikizela-Mandela

Even though the fullness of his excitement was hidden behind his mask, I could still read his eyes, and they revealed his truth. With a freshly printed schedule in hand, and a new backpack without wear or tear strapped to his back, he nervously, yet confidently handed me his "passport" and said, "I'm in your homeroom."

After asking his name and a few other welcoming

and qualifying questions, I asked Brandon if he was joining us from another school or if he was switching over from the virtual platform. He said, "I was virtual, but that wasn't working for me." With those words, I was able to make the connection. What I had seen in Brandon's eyes made sense. The revelation was instant.

Relief.

Expectation.

Joy automatically triggered by gaining a long-awaited admittance into a new land. Hope for a fresh start and a new way of life.

I didn't immediately point Brandon to a seat in the classroom. Instead, I invited him to remain with me in the hallway as I welcomed students into the building and ushered them through the morning bustle to their homerooms. I wanted to chat with him and know more about what I'd seen in his eyes.

Later, after homeroom, once class was in session, it was apparent that Brandon was hungry not only for face-to-face instruction, but interaction with his peers. There wasn't a question I asked that his hand wasn't flying up to answer; every word I uttered had his full attention. Then, in the middle of the student work session, when students were prompted to talk to their assigned partners in socially distanced stance—standing outside of their desks that sit six feet apart, facing each other with masks fully covering both mouth and nose—he was the first one on his feet. Students who had been in face-to-face instruction since the start of the school year, for roughly six weeks, were bored with the talk-to-your-partner routine. They'd done it a number of times. There was no more excitement in it for them. But Brandon couldn't wait. It was fresh and new to him. It was what he'd been missing. It was what he'd been longing for. He hadn't had any peer-to-peer classroom interaction for seven months, and that day, he soaked up every minute of it. He allowed himself to fully absorb every new experience.

It was a joy to witness.

And Brandon is just one example. Other students who

returned to face-to-face instruction in January 2021, after a full semester of virtual learning, exhibited similar behaviors. Quite telling, I'd say.

When the coronavirus began its international trek, touching down in the United States in February 2020, spreading more rapidly than could be managed or even understood, schools across the country shut down without question or a second thought. Clearly, it's what was best for everyone's safety. For many school districts, the ones that were able to muster technological prowess to keep teachers and students afloat, the 2019-2020 school year ended virtually. But regardless of districts' ability to forge ahead with online instruction or not, the abrupt shift took the world of education on a ride like none it's ever experienced. It was the world's hope that the pandemic would be short lived, but after February came March, and after March, April, with the pandemic firmly hovering. In fact, as May, June, and July came and went, COVID cases and the death toll continued to rise, making it devastatingly clear that school wouldn't be "back to normal" in August.

School districts had to decide if they would go completely virtual or not for the 2020-2021 school year. Surveys went out to families to gauge their desires for how the school year should proceed. As much as possible, school districts attempted to do what was best for everyone. Some districts decided to go completely virtual. Others chose hybrid models where students would attend face-to-face classes a couple days a week, and virtual classes at home the other days. Some districts did a complete face-to-face model, and some, like ours, the Richmond County School System (RCSS), had both the face-to-face and completely virtual models in full operation all school year.

Having had the opportunity to see both models in action means having seen, up close and personal, the woes and glows with both. Unfortunately, the woes outweigh the glows. The virtual teachers complained of having students enrolled in their classes who never—not one day—logged onto the online school system. They regularly spoke of student apathy and the lack of student participation in class. Their biggest complaint, though, was students' failing grades.

One of the 8th grade teachers who taught 7th graders the 2019-2020 school year had a unique scope. In one faculty meeting, she shared with the staff that some of the A students she'd had as 7th graders were earning D's and F's in her virtual class. She knew those students to be intelligent, self-starting hard workers. She knew what they were capable of, but no matter what she tried, many of them she couldn't motivate to perform at their maximum potential. One of those students was Brandon. Brandon hadn't made an A on one assignment in the virtual teacher's class, but *every* assignment he completed in my class earned an A with little to no effort.

When Brandon and I had a talk one day, again, in the hallway before homeroom, I asked him what was so different about virtual instruction. He said he didn't feel like he was being taught with virtual instruction. He said it seemed like his teachers talked about the work instead of teaching it. The workload, he explained, was unnecessarily heavy, and even though there were class meetings, it just wasn't the same. He admitted that he couldn't stay focused, no matter what he tried. He had realized, after only three weeks in virtual instruction, that he needed a classroom. He couldn't flourish at home. Students who returned to the school building in January had the same sentiments. They applauded RCSS for even having the virtual learning option available for students, but they were forthright in expressing their need to be in a classroom, engaging with other students, with their hands on the material they were learning, and with direct, physical access to a teacher.

Brandon had only been in face-to-face instruction nine days when our school had to be shut down for two weeks for COVID concerns. While out, we carried on with a virtual schedule on the Canvas online platform that the district adopted. At the beginning of the school year, every student in the school received in depth instruction on how to navigate the system in the event a shutdown went into effect. We even had times in class where we worked on assignments in the system. It was our school's goal to make sure students were prepared.

Over that two-week period, Brandon did one of six
assignments, and he didn't show up for any of the
virtual class sessions. He didn't respond to any emails
that questioned his absences or incomplete
assignments, and he removed himself from every one
of his teachers' Remind App update lists.

Naturally, upon return from the 2-week hiatus,
Brandon and I had a conversation. It had become
our thing. He explained that he just chose not to do
the work because he had done all he was going to
do with virtual assignments. Willing to take whatever
grade he earned, he was just ready to pick up with
school and forget about all things virtual. He didn't
want to think about it, and he definitely didn't want
to talk about it. That had been our shortest
conversation in the time that we'd known each
other.

Virtual had left a sour taste in his mouth. Was he able
to do the work? Yes. Was he willing to do it? No.
And can we blame him?

Our school body, unfortunately, was out of the building more in the 2020-2021 school year than it was in the building. And in 8th grade's case, because of COVID exposure in Brandon's class, the entire class had to be out for a week that other 8th graders didn't have to be out. It was a rollercoaster for him, to say the least.

Every time we had to close the school for COVID concerns, there was less than 25% of students to complete assignments, and less than 15% to show up for class meetings. I like to think they all had Brandon's mindset. They had signed up for face-to-face learning. They hadn't signed up for virtual. When they were made to engage in virtual instruction, it was stressful. It was too much independent work when they were accustomed to working with a teacher and with peers. They knew they needed to be inside a classroom because they knew that's how they would excel.

They were tired.
They felt cheated.

They wanted to learn.

They wanted some normalcy.

Teachers felt it too.

They were tired of the back and forth. They were tired of having to take what they were teaching and put it into a virtual platform. They were tired of living on the edge of their seats, wondering if they'd get to see projects through to the end without interruption. Teachers were losing hope too. They wondered if it would always be that way. They, alongside their students, wondered if all would be lost.

CHECKLIST: SOCIAL-EMOTIONAL SUPPORTS

☐ HAS EVERY MEMBER OF THE FACULTY AND STAFF PARTICIPATED IN PROFESSIONAL LEARNING ON SOCIAL-EMOTIONAL LEARNING?

☐ ARE MORNING MEETINGS IMPLEMENTED SCHOOL-WIDE WITH FIDELITY? DO MEMBERS OF THE LEADERSHIP TEAM REGULARLY DROP IN TO OBSERVE THE MEETINGS? IS THE MORNING MEETING REFERENCED ON THE LESSON PLANS?

☐ DOES THE SCHOOL COUNSELING TEAM HAVE AN ESTABLISHED CALENDAR TO VISIT CLASSES AND PROVIDE LESSONS ON S.E.L. TOPICS TO STUDENTS?

☐ HAS A MENTORING SYSTEM BEEN ESTABLISHED TO SUPPORT STUDENTS WHO ARE STRUGGLING WITH ACADEMICS, ATTENDANCE, OR SOCIAL CHALLENGES? DO MEMBERS OF OUR STAFF SPONSOR EXTRA-CURRICULAR ACTIVITIES FOR OUR SCHOLARS?

☐ HAVE ONGOING PARTNERSHIPS BEEN ESTABLISHED WITH COMMUNITY AGENCIES TO SUPPORT S.E.L. WORK IN OUR SCHOOL? DO THESE PARTNERSHIPS HELP TO PROVIDE RESOURCES SUCH AS FOOD, CLOTHING, SHELTER, AND COUNSELING FOR FAMILIES?

☐ DO ANNOUNCEMENTS AND POSTERS IN OUR SCHOOL REFLECT S.E.L. THEMES SUCH AS RESILIENCE, HUMILITY, INTEGRITY, SELF-CONTROL, AND COURAGE?

☐ DOES THE SCHOOL ADMINISTRATION ACTIVELY ATTEND TO THE SOCIAL-EMOTIONAL NEEDS OF THE FACULTY AND STAFF BY DISCUSSING SELF-CARE, WELLNESS, AND ACTS OF GRATITUDE (I.E.: GIFTS, NOTES, KUDOS, SHOUT-OUTS, AWARDS)?

©DEF-ED 2021

André Benito Mountain

Chapter 7: In A *Virtual* Way

By André Benito Mountain Principal

"I am invisible, understand, simply because people refuse to see me."
-Ralph Ellison in "Invisible Man

I t was 1987. I was awakened during the middle of the night by the sounds of tambourines, drums, and syncopated wailings from the park at the intersection of King Circle Drive and Norwood Avenue in Swainsboro, Georgia. Those sounds were a mixture of African rhythms and Southern blues with an overlay of guttural shouts from a preacher pleading that the congregates praise God in their shouting. At times I'd hear over twenty-five consecutive bars of "Hallelujah! Praise him!" If you've never experienced the sound and feel of a Holiness Revival in a tent in the American South, you have yet to witness something that, for an eight-year-old, was both terrifying and fascinating. These revival camps intended to bring about instantaneous conversions and resurrection of the spirit. During those late-night revivals, I experienced an instantaneous conversion from sleep to alertness and rose from my bed on the third song. I'd begin peeling back the blanket and shuffling across the hardwood floors to the window to get a glimpse of what I was hearing. Outside my window, I could see a large white tent with a soft yellow glow of lamps inside casting shadows of people jumping up and down the sides of the tent.

America is in its awakening and revival that is both terrifying and fascinating. The country is begrudgingly awakening to an awareness of the deep crevices in our democracy that have been salient in the lives of Black people for decades if not centuries in this country. Political disenfranchisement and police brutality are not new issues for us. We've shouted, wailed, sang, and marched in hopes that there would be an instantaneous conversion of our communities, schools, and society. Could it have taken the shuttering of our schools and an incompetent presidency to bring us to the point of looking out the window to see what's happening?

When this started in the Spring of 2020, it felt as
though the education profession was virtually lost, left
to find its way with no guidance from the top levels of
the educational bureaucracy. We did not look to
Betsy Devos for direction because her lack of
concern for public education had already been
proven. We are a profession that is present, but
unseen and unacknowledged, like the invisible man
in Ralph Ellison's 1947 novel of the same name.
Written one year before the birth of my parents, the
novel depicts the world into which they were being
born where Black bodies were present, but not
readily seen. Little has changed. He writes, "I am
invisible, understand, simply because people refuse
to see me." Incrementally, that refusal to see the
education profession ended when schools no longer
served their perhaps tertiary purpose of housing
children away from the home.

Generational forces are pulling on schools like
constellations creating certain energy with which
they are forced to contend. Underfunding of schools
in the areas of technology and class sizes is a
nationwide issue. Adequately staffing schools with

enough administrators and support staff to deliver effective professional development and to manage the endless flow of paperwork needed to run a school is a concern that needs attention from the federal level. It is in these finite moments that leaders both find and define themselves like jazz musicians singing their versions of a standard like Brooks Bowman's "East of the Sun and West of the Moon". The familiar becomes unfamiliar with an approach that is uniquely Sinatra, Ella, or Armstrong. Though the words on the page are identical, the way it is delivered is where the magic lies.

East of the Sun and West of the Moon

Mrs. Moon has always been an involved and supportive member of our school community. She was a few years into her retirement, but still very active in our school community. She could be found volunteering, helping with our school garden, and leading fundraising initiatives in the lobby of our school. The entire Moon family was beloved by our school's faculty and staff. Last Fall, we encountered a bit of a rift as Mrs. Moon had a granddaughter entering 5th grade. She was insistent that her granddaughter be placed in Mr. Day's homeroom class. He was a widely popular and gregarious teacher whose passion for teaching was evident to families. Classes had already been constructed and I was strictly against the 'teacher shopping' practice many families engaged in each year at many schools, campaigning for their child to be placed in a certain classroom. Complicating matters was the frequent back and forth of guardianship in some households, making it difficult to determine exactly who was in the position to make educational decisions from month to month. I tried to explain to Mrs. Moon that even though Mr. Day was not her granddaughter's homeroom teacher that she'd still have Mr. Day for instruction during the school day.

"Mrs. Moon, we've already placed her in a class, and while it's not Mr. Day's class, I can assure you that she'll have a wonderful experience this year."

Displeased with my response, she replied, "I'm gonna just have to do what I have to do."

I wondered what the phrase meant in this context. Clarity came the next day when I was informed that she was contemplating withdrawing all three children from the school because I wouldn't grant her request to place this one child in a certain classroom. She kept them out of school for a week, but suddenly they reappeared, and the withdrawal was never fully completed. Honestly, I was glad she had a change of heart. These were great scholars, and this was a family that had been with us for years. I wanted to see them stay, but not at the cost of compromising the integrity of how we place scholars in classes. The educator is an artist, and his practice is his portrait. The job of the artist as an educator is not to create what the public wants to hear, see, or read. The job of the artist as an educator is to create what he is compelled to create that aligns with who he is and what the moment calls for one to create. Once one begins to compromise the integrity of the work, they compromise larger aspects of the profession.

This year, like many of our scholars, the Moons are in a living room on their devices, engaging in virtual learning. Mrs. Moon is holding court as the teacher on special assignment in a satellite campus, trouble-shooting IT issues and connecting with teachers at different grade levels and different schools. She is a grandmother and honorary teacher, trying to ensure that each of her grandchildren gets the best educational experience they can in a virtual setting. It's not what she wanted. It's not what we wanted. It is what we've been presented within an unprecedented global pandemic. It is disjointed and unnatural. It is mechanical and aseptic. It is a school experience being offered in a virtual way.

Playing As We've Never Played Before

The story of the Moon family is a case study of what is happening on a large scale in our schools today. One wonders where the parents are as the grandparents essentially raise a second generation in an age where school looks fundamentally different from anything we've ever experienced before. The Baby Boomers, born between the 1940s and the 1960s, have been dealt an unfair hand in their retirement years by Generation X. Left with their grandchildren to raise, many of them are the regular attendees at our school events, parent conferences, or PTA meetings. During the pandemic, it has been the combined impact of the lack of technology and technical aptitude that has exacerbated the digital divide and the subsequent achievement gap for inner-city youth. In more tragic instances, children are left to raise themselves or one another as the parents leave them home alone so they can work during this pandemic. The need for food clothing and shelter has not paused for one moment since schools have closed.

On February 18, 1969, in CBS's 30th Street Studio, Miles Davis sat in a studio with a set of musicians and began recording his album "In a Silent Way". This album and the title song were a shift from his previous work in that it marked his move to electric instrumentation. It was a point where he was integrating more technology into his recordings. As the details of the title track were being worked out, Miles was trying to describe how he wanted John McLaughlin to lead into the piece on the guitar. He told him to "play like he didn't know how to play". What we hear is a slow, deliberate, hesitant style of play that pulls the listener into the tune with anticipation for what the other musicians will add to the tune. It is unorthodox. It is counter-intuitive given the sound we have come to know as Miles on previous albums. Miles has taught us, with his horn and with his style of leadership, that we must always leave room for changing lanes. Change always makes us uncomfortable. It is inevitable and necessary. The album "In a Silent Way" broke barriers. Rolling Stone described it as "the kind of album that gives you faith in the future of music."

Perhaps this moment is just what needed to happen to bring our attention to the many needed changes in the field of public education. Veterans and early career teachers are all being forced to teach as they've never taught before.

Now, as we begin to welcome students back into the classrooms, we are asking teachers to provide concurrent learning. This marks the second shift they've made in the format of teaching since the pandemic began. We must be responsive to the stress this places upon teachers and provide as much support and flexibility as needed to facilitate this transition. Our schools can't afford to lose talented and dedicated educators at a time when they are the cornerstone of the entire school.

CHECKLIST: CONCURRENT LEARNING

☐ HAS PROFESSIONAL DEVELOPMENT BEEN PROVIDED TO HELP TEACHERS UNDERSTAND HOW TO DELIVER EFFECTIVE CONCURRENT LEARNING?

☐ HAS THE SCHOOL LEADERSHIP IDENTIFIED TEACHER LEADERS TO SUPPORT GRADE LEVELS ON ASPECTS OF CONCURRENT LEARNING INCLUDING ASSESSMENT, STUDENT ENGAGEMENT, AND NAVIGATING PLATFORMS?

☐ HAVE PARENT MEETINGS BEEN HELD TO ASSIST PARENTS IN NAVIGATING VIRTUAL LEARNING PLATFORMS?

☐ DO TEACHERS HAVE A CLEAR UNDERSTANDING OF HOW TO PROVIDE A DIFFERENT EXPERIENCE FOR STUDENTS WHO ARE IN-PERSON VERSUS THOSE WHO ARE LEARNING VIRTUALLY?

☐ DO MEMBERS OF THE SCHOOL COMMUNITY HAVE A CLEAR UNDERSTANDING OF THE TERMS 'CONCURRENT LEARNING', 'VIRTUAL LEARNING', AND 'HYBRID INSTRUCTION'?

☐ DO MEMBERS OF THE SCHOOL LEADERSHIP TEAM REGULARLY PROVIDE FEEDBACK ON THE QUALITY OF INSTRUCTION, SPECIFICALLY REFERENCING HOW CONCURRENT LEARNING IS BEING IMPLEMENTED?

André Benito Mountain

Chapter 8: Chronicles of Formal Education: Being Better Prepared

By Iantha Ussin
Educator

The history of formal education in the United States has been consistently recorded since its inception in the 1800s. Americans have never had to wonder about what was happening in schools. Every trend, every happening, every practice, and every policy—the good, the bad, and the ugly—documented, allowing us to trace how different sectors in education have evolved over time, and how others have either stagnated or completely died. Regardless of the direction of the change, the face of education has had its share.

In 1954, for example, the ruling in the landmark Supreme Court case, Brown vs. Board of Education, declared "separate-but-equal" education unconstitutional, allowing children of all races, for the first time in American history, to go to school together. This triumphant upheaval was one of many that simultaneously rallied against segregation of every kind, on every level, throughout the Civil Rights Movement. Pivotal and powerful, the Supreme Court decision changed the face of education and stood as a pillar to proclaim that separate was not in fact equal.

The Individuals with Disabilities Education Act (IDEA) was instituted in 1975, allowing children with disabilities to have an appropriate public education with any necessary accommodations and related services to ensure it. Yet another triumph for equality in education.

Then, the No Child Left Behind Act (NCLB) in 2001, instated with the goal of improving student success through annual standardized assessments, made schools aware of, and responsible for their students' academic performance. NCLB forever changed the way schools offer instruction, causing there to be a widespread overall increase in students' academic success.

It has all been chronicled. We know all there is to know about the wins in education. And we know about the losses too.

Although the rash of school shootings (massacres in some cases) that swept the country between1999 and 2019 weren't initiated by any schools, the shooters *did* target schools, which inadvertently, and quite unfortunately, connected school and all it entails to fear, death, and loss.

> Any wholesome view of school, or education itself, tainted.
> Its positive light, dimmed.
> Faculty, staff, and students, afraid to trust the hallways again.
> Parents apprehensive about "releasing their children to the wild".
> Schools arming themselves with millions of dollars of preparation and activation training, and new safety technologies to keep all stakeholders protected.

Every bit of it was covered by some media source and because of the advancement of technology, cell phones were able to capture some live video and audio footage of intrusions. Nothing like it had ever been seen in schools, an almost unspeakable "happening" in education.

Then, in 2020, after a period of silence from mass shootings, the coronavirus made an appearance.

> A global pandemic.
> Businesses and major corporations completely incapacitated.
> Air travel and public transportation, at every level, suspended.
> Schools shut down, almost without notice.

And again, just like every other pivotal point in history that had some direct effect on education, it was documented. Virtual instruction and its impact on students and families was the major longstanding headline in education news, beginning in March 2020. Other discussions made headlines too, like

'Should Students Return to School?' and 'Will Standardized Tests Have a Place in the 2020-2021 School Year?' But there has never been an in-depth chronicling of how educators—the ones in the trenches, on the front lines with students—feel about the effects the pandemic has had on instruction, student-teacher relationships, and education as a whole.

Until now.

This time in the life of education shouldn't be devoid of reflections from the educators themselves. André knew this. The only way the world will really know about the "happenings" in education during the coronavirus pandemic is if they hear it from the voices of the ones to which it happened. Andre` specializes in capturing pertinent moments in history, packaging them in palatable artistic forms, and presenting them with excellence, fidelity, and clarity. This book is one shining example. His experience and expertise as a proven, ranked educator and three-time author afford him the right to have written Virtually Lost himself, but the message, he knows, is louder with the collection of voices—his and other educators—that have contributed to this work.

André sprang into action because the principal in him, who sees and hears the daily cries of his faculty and staff, couldn't allow them to go unheard. The world needs to go into the classrooms with teachers who returned to their school buildings and see what they saw and feel what they felt. The world needs to experience the school day with these teachers—the joys, the pains, the uncertainties, the little glimmers of hope, *and* the lack thereof. The world needs to log on and walk with teachers through a day of virtual instruction to experience all the ups and all the downs.

As the saying goes, *"History repeats itself."* It's true, but it doesn't necessarily have to be. That's one of the reasons for this compilation. In the event that the world experiences another pandemic or anything else that triggers an abrupt shut down for schools, we'll know what worked. We'll know what didn't work. We'll know how to be proactive. We'll know how to gauge students and teachers' social and emotional health thermometers. School districts won't have to scramble to figure things out and can already have systems and practices in place. With a tool like this in their hands, they can better prepare. They will have heard it from the horses' mouths, and with that, they can maybe prevent being virtually lost.

André Benito Mountain

Chapter 9: Losing Their Voices

By André Benito Mountain Principal

The bonds that exist between educators and families in small towns are unmatched in larger metropolitan cities. The tenures are more stable and a faculty's community connections are as deep as family ties . It was 1983. Mrs. Doyle watched us file into her classroom as she clutched a handful of worksheets behind her back. She stood squarely at top of the stairs looking down on us over her horn-rimmed glasses which typically hung from a beaded lanyard around her neck. In her right hand was her yardstick. It was not the regular yardstick that my mother used to measure fabric when she was making a dress from a pattern. Mrs. Doyle's yardstick had more girth and its function was not for measuring. While she never used it as a teaching manipulative for mathematics, it was used to increase student engagement and participation. *It was her scepter*. It was thy rod and thy staff that did not comfort us in any shape or fashion, but only offered chastisement, binding and casting out the spirit of disobedience when it settled amongst us. She was an older African-American woman with small moles underneath her eyes like my grandparents. Mrs. Doyle was more like a grandmother to us than a teacher.

She'd taught many of our parents, so there was no room for any of us to "run home to tell on the teacher" in those days. Our parents knew how Mrs. Doyle ran her class and we all understood that there was no one coming to rescue us from her if we didn't meet her expectations for behavior or academic excellence. She never sent anyone to the office and never paused our instructional time to write a discipline referral. Our days were busy with working on our handwriting, revising verb tenses, and perfecting pronoun usage. We remained with Mrs. Doyle all day and she taught us how I imagined children were taught in the days of the one-room schoolhouse. We were her children while we were there. That meant something. She was an extension of our parents' and grandparents' belief in order, structure, and intolerance for foolishness. She was both judge and jury in that portable classroom that sat on a portion of the large playground at Swainsboro Primary School. In that portable though, no games were being played.

I asked my mother, a retired high school teacher, when she saw a shift in students during her teaching career. She said that there came a point during the 1990s when she began to hear of parents who wanted to come to the school in a rage to "fight and curse out" the teachers because of what a student said. It was a change from the respect she'd seen given to teachers during the first part of her career. She began to see a generation of parents whose primary aim was to defend the behavior of the child at all costs rather than allow the child to be held accountable. The teacher's voice began to fade behind that of the child, the parent, and the district. Teachers were losing their voices.

My brother and I never had the luxury of having our parents come to the school to defend our misbehavior. Jimmie and Marie Mountain made it abundantly clear that they were not our friends. When my mother would say, "That teacher better not call me", it was not a warning being issued to the teacher or the school. It was a warning for us to "govern ourselves and act accordingly." We'd been birthed into a school setting that was only a few generations removed from the independent church schools and one-room schoolhouses that littered the south during Reconstruction. My class was all-Black, but my school was racially integrated. If you'd ask me where the children of other races were, I'd have to assume that they were assigned to classrooms inside the building. During those years, I only recall seeing White students during recess, lunch, or during dismissal. The structure of our school was an echo of an unspoken culture in our town that affected every aspect of life including real estate, school bus routes, Sunday worship, and the type of education we received.

"Sit down and be quiet! Mountain, pass out these papers."

"Yes ma'am."

She handed me the papers and they had that damp feel that the worksheets always had when she'd just left the teacher's lounge. I sniffed the stack and smelled that familiar smell. We never knew what it was, but we liked it. There was nothing quite like a 'wet stack' of copies. Nearly everyone sniffed their papers as I went up and down the rows of wooden desks. The smell on those damp papers was from the fluid in the risograph machine which consisted of methanol, a highly toxic chemical used to make antifreeze, and isopropanol, a key ingredient in rubbing alcohol. After everyone got their fix, I handed the remainder of the papers back to Mrs. Doyle and took my seat near the rear of the room. In those days, teachers would create a 'master copy' by hand, crafting sentences, drawing blanks, and writing questions that we would have to respond to in complete sentences. She used the risograph to make 30 copies of her hand-crafted activities. We'd be tasked with writing our words as neatly as she'd done on the master copy. If it didn't meet her standard, you were quickly dispatched back to your seat to make another go at it.

Technology always has a way of being bittersweet in the end. The introduction of the risograph and other types of copy machines in the 80s was no different. The risograph itself was not a problem. The way the risograph would eventually be used became problematic for the profession. The purple pigment on those papers was the new blood being pumped into the teaching profession, gradually transfusing out the creativity and autonomy of teachers. My generation unknowingly witnessed educational euthanasia at the hands of publishers with glossy and colorful teacher editions and workbooks that would in the coming years supplant Mrs. Doyle's handcrafted lessons with scripts for teachers and worksheets that corresponded with the units she was assigned to teach.

Education at its best is a *gumbo* where relationships, collaboration, motivational theory, and relevance are among the ingredients, but the artistry of the teacher is the irreplaceable *roux*.

Educational Ventriloquism

Those worksheets she created were extensions of Mrs. Doyle's creativity, duplicated for us all to complete. Later, publishers would supplant even this practice by providing schools with workbooks and worksheets that, by the mid to late 80s, would constitute much of what we did during the school day. Teaching moves in the classes I would join would become increasingly scripted. Planning a lesson was now as easy as preparing a bowl of Jello or a pan of StoveTop stuffing. Little or no planning is required, just add risograph fluid. Publishing companies were performing educational ventriloquism as the unseen hands turning the pages of the teachers' editions and determining what we'd learn next. America's teachers are too talented to be limited by the strings of publishing puppeteers. Principals and teachers have to find common ground and fight to ensure the artistry of education is preserved. While some of our teachers resisted this wave of educational ventriloquism, others saw it as a way to save them the time and stress of preparing lessons and further the agenda of absolute standardization.

Irreplaceable Roux

Creativity in public education has been under assault for decades. The newest incarnations of weapons of mass instruction include the many prescriptive programs that promise to increase scores by assigning specific lessons, Teachers Pay Teachers, and workbooks that promise to prepare scholars to ace the upcoming assessments. None of these new developments are more impactful than the vision and innovation of a committed teacher. They only enhance the pedagogical gifts a teacher brings into the classroom just as a pair of athletic shoes enhance the performance of a gifted athlete on a soccer field. Are teachers losing their voices behind instructional materials? Are they able to hear and see themselves or are they being drowned out by the prepackaged resources they use? Is the profession D.O.A. - Devoid of artistry? Teachers entering the profession must understand that our work is much more than mastering the tips, tricks, and techniques of instruction. It is the wisdom of knowing when to play a note, repeat a note, bask in silence, and stand on a table. The preparation of the ingredients before a lesson is served is as much a part of the artistry of education as is the delivery of the lesson. Pupils are our patrons whose tastes are more inclined toward the eclectic than the efficient. At a moment when we are forced to decide whether schools should be reopened, are we listening to the voice of our teachers? Have we placed our teachers on mute or made them fear for their jobs to the point where they've muted themselves from the discussions about reopening schools at the height of a global pandemic? Education at its best is a *gumbo* where relationships, collaboration, motivational theory, and relevance are among the ingredients, but the artistry of the teacher is the irreplaceable *roux*.

CHECKLIST:
LIFTING TEACHERS' VOICES

☐ DO GRADE LEVEL CHAIRS HAVE A CLEAR AGENDA OF TOPICS TO INCLUDE IN GRADE-LEVEL MEETINGS AND COLLABORATIVE PLANING THAT ALIGN TO SCHOOL IMPROVEMENT GOALS?

☐ HAVE PROTOCOLS BEEN ESTABLISHED FOR TEACHERS TO OFFER INPUT ON ISSUES THAT HAVE SCHOOL-WIDE IMPACT?

☐ WHEN PLANS ARE PRESENTED TO THE STAFF, ARE THERE OPPORTUNITIES FOR TEACHERS TO POSE CLARIFYING QUESTIONS ABOUT THE PLANS?

☐ ARE TEACHERS ENCOURAGED TO ATTEND SCHOOL BOARD MEETINGS IN-PERSON OR VIRTUALLY TO REMAIN INFORMED ABOUT DISTRICT DECISIONS THAT AFFECT THEIR WORK?

☐ HAS THE SCHOOL ESTABLISHED A SCHOOL LEADERSHIP TEAM WHICH INCLUDES TEACHER AND PARAPROFESSIONAL REPRESENTATIVES?

☐ DOES THE SCHOOL ADMINISTRATION DEMONSTRATE A WILLINGNESS TO CONSIDER TEACHERS' CONCERNS AND SUGGESTIONS BY MODIFYING PROTOCOLS AND PROCEDURES BASED ON TEACHER FEEDBACK? WHAT IS THE EVIDENCE OF THIS?

☐ IS THERE A REGULAR INTEGRATED DIAGNOSTIC OR COMPREHENSIVE SURVEY PROVIDED TO TEACHERS TO MEASURE THEIR BELIEFS ABOUT MULTIPLE ASPECTS OF THE SCHOOL'S OVERALL OPERATIONS AND ACADEMIC STRUCTURES?

André Benito Mountain

Chapter 10: Yoruba Twins

By André Benito Mountain
Principal

The discussion of the role of the arts in public education has become virtually lost in light of the school closings due to the global pandemic. Many of our scholars find their greatest joy in those moments when they are able to freely create in art and music classrooms. Art and education can be seen as twins, born from the same womb. In the Yoruba tradition, the name "Kehinde" means "the second born of the twins". The second born twin is considered the elder twin. The first twin, Taiwo, emerges into the world, determining whether the conditions are right to be born. Only then is Kehinde birthed.

Education is Taiwo.

The arts are Kehinde.

In May of 2016, my family took the escalator to the featured exhibit floor of the Seattle Art Museum to view the exhibit of <u>Kehinde Wiley</u>. An artist who describes himself as a descendant in art history's portrait painting tradition, his works place Black men and women in heroic and aristocratic scenes, drawing inspiration from the Western tradition of portraiture with a notable celebration of African features. His palette and technique are drawn from the wellspring of classical paintings of noblemen and royalty, noting that his goal is "to be able to paint illusionistically and master the technical aspects, but then to be able to fertilize that with great ideas." His works accomplish what great art and music have always done: *force us to confront socio-political contradictions and issues of race, gender and power.*

Four years after visiting Wiley's exhibit in Seattle, the art teacher at our metro-Atlanta school introduced our elementary scholars to the works of <u>Kehinde Wiley</u>, tasking them with creating their own self-portraits inspired by his works. It was our effort to create a culturally responsive space for our scholars to experience the works of a contemporary artist and to grapple with the task of reconceptualizing the past in a way that asserts new ideas upon it. Walter Benjamin once wrote, "In every era the attempt must be made to wrest tradition away from a conformist that is about to overpower it." The catalysts of changing the institutional forces working to devalue the arts in our schools are the educators and leaders who understand the intellectual complexity of creating art and the implications for fostering greater creativity in our schools.

We find a similar duality in Hip-Hop culture as artists grapple with its legacy of social change, authenticity and lyricism, along with the missteps, materialism and misogyny. Lyric Jones represents a countercurrent of contemporary artists who strive to create Hip-Hop compositions in a way that honors the tradition. Her most recent album, Closer Than They Appear, gazes into Hip-Hop's rearview mirror while steadily moving the culture forward with tracks like "Rock On" and

"Cruisin". Like Kehinde Wiley, she too, stands in a lyrical line of descendants that includes Pete Rock and CL Smooth, Big Daddy Kane, Souls of Mischief, Lauryn Hill and Little Brother. Jones captures the essence of this in her song "Rock On" where she confesses:

"I kept tally
Of every small to big victory
Even when Hip Hop grew more contradictory
Still was at the pep rally
Cause I marvel at the history"

Lyric Jones' work epitomizes where the arts, education, culture and context converge. She references her joint enrollment and experiences in summer programs at the Berklee College of Music in her hometown of Boston as instrumental in her development as an artist. She possesses a transcendent level of skill, engaging in production, singing, songwriting, and drumming. She IS the culture embodied. What is most significant for the future of the culture is the fact that she is also an educator at the Musicians Institute's College of Contemporary Music.

In our mission to create schools that leverage the arts to unleash the genius we see in both Wiley and Jones, we must first reassess what it means to teach, what is taught, and what is valued in schools in the frantic "race to the top". I acknowledge that what happens in the classrooms, whether in person or virtual, is most critical. But I would suggest that we start our assessment of the relationship between the arts and education at the front doors of our schools. The lobby of a school tells the story of a school. Too often the visual cues of the vestibules of our schools are overlooked. They are indicative of what is valued in a space. Here we discover, long before our interaction with its citizenry, whether athletics, academics, alumni or the arts are held in high regard. The critical thinking skills and differentiation we espouse as we discuss raising student achievement in the core content areas is not the same brush used to paint the arts in our schools. The arts are currently underfunded in our schools and relegated to second-class status in relation to other content areas. This is a problem that must be addressed at the federal level of education. We've arrived at this point in public education after a series of education reform efforts that included measurements of progress in specific subjects, causing administrators and policymakers to trim budgets and streamline their offerings to align with what was measurable on standardized tests.

Education must confront its own contradictions. Blooms Taxonomy was revised in 2001 by a consortium of psychologists, curriculum theorists, and educational researchers. It illustrates the cognitive processes and the continuum of complexity of tasks from 'remember' to 'create'. According to Blooms, 'create' represents the highest form of cognitive activity. This is where we find students generating a log of activities, assembling a team of experts, designing a project workflow, or developing a learning portfolio. Elliot Eisner, in a 1969 article entitled "What the Arts Taught Me About Education", suggests that the complexity of painting "requires the exercise of the mind...and the process of perceiving the subtleties of a work of art is as much of an inquiry as the design of an experiment in chemistry."

We are called upon to widen our conceptualization of what it means to be smart. Reconstruction of this concept necessitates the dismantling of the notion that education, at its core, is limited to the importation of that which can be measured by standardized tests. Dismantling this requires an examination of the core of university programs that prepare our teachers and our teacher leaders.

Audre Lorde

Audre Lorde, in her critique of feminists during her time once wrote "The master's tools will never dismantle the master's house." Her quote reminds us that reforming institutions from within can be a challenging undertaking. To be employed within, and at times bound by the bureaucracy of public education, yet possessing a keen knowledge of its ongoing toxicity and disservice to our young people who are predominantly Black, and Brown is both an invocation to self-determination and an invitation to the dance between compliance and creativity. Elliot Eisner, in looking back on his experiences as a student and the sacredness of the visual arts during his elementary years, describes the visual arts as a source of 'salvation' from the drudgery of diagramming sentences in English grammar classes.

As educators, we most often focus our professional expertise on how the context of schooling transforms scholars. The context of schooling also transforms those of us working in schools, peeling away layers of lingo, acronyms, and new initiatives. Leaving us alone in our classrooms engaged in our own personal quests to impact the lives of our scholars. We become more connected with our sacred selves. As Eisner describes his first experiences teaching art in Chicago Public Schools, he formulates an intricate mosaic bound together by a deep commitment to both art and education. He suggests that the context and the content have transformative potentiality, writing:

"Chicago also provided the theoretical tools and the intellectual climate that I needed; much of it was like my life as a child at home; ideas were prized almost for their own sake. Analysis, debate, and intellect had a happy marriage."

-Elliot Eisner

Eisner's pericope on the context of his own transformative experience with art and education is much like my own experience as a school leader intent on exploring the voids that exist between the arts and core content courses.

As I first walked into the metro-Atlanta school I had been chosen to lead as principal, I looked intently at the hallways and what adorned its walls. I wanted to get an understanding of the culture of the school and the community through what was posted. It was April, yet some of the work posted was dated from November of the previous year. Framed artwork was hanging in many locations throughout the building, honoring the legacy of African-American history and culture. I wondered why the energy, creativity, and excitement of the hundreds of students of the school wasn't more prominently displayed around the campus. Three years later, our halls are adorned with art created by scholars in class. Hallway displays include project-based learning and student writings. We have become much more intentional about presenting scholars with complex tasks to broaden their own sense of self-efficacy. Eisner challenges the prevailing culture of public education, writing, "educational practice does not display its highest virtues in uniformity, but in nurturing productive diversity." There is complexity in a musical score or in sixteen bars of rap lyrics. There is intellect and critical thinking at the forefront of a painting. There is genius in the choreography that accompanies a Jazz composition. As a school leader, I'm interested in finding ways to initiate that sense of "salvation" Eisner describes for those students who have developed a dread for other content areas. The city of Atlanta has become the nexus of an African-American Renaissance where artistic virtuosity emerges from every corner of the city. It is a place where one can walk in the footsteps of W.E.B. DuBois and Dr. Martin

Luther King Jr. Community artists and activists are found leaving indelible marks on the city through their work in schools and on murals. We now have the opportunity to re-envision schools as spaces where the arts are repositioned in the instructional hierarchy. Instead of the arts standing in the periphery, let's explore how the arts can sit at the center of all we do in our schools.

Chapter 11: Belmont Runyon Elementary School, Newark, NJ

By Cassandra Carson, Heidi Cruz, Rhonda Gordon, Tonya Ingram, Pamela Hunter, Mitchell Summers

How has the pandemic impacted education from your perspective?

This chapter contains essays from six Special Education Teachers from Belmont Runyon Elementary School in Newark, NJ's South Ward working with moderate to severe cognitive impaired students.

As an educator teaching in the South Ward of Newark NJ, the pandemic has really affected the educational progress of our children. It has widened the learning gap that many of our children were already experiencing. When the schools were forced to shut down, students whose families were of higher economic status were able to financially utilize the outside resources to support their child's education during the school's closing. Unlike their peers whose parents may not have had the same privilege were left to figure it out. This crisis has exposed the many inadequacies and inequities in our education systems. Even within my school, many students didn't have access to the broadband and computers needed for online education, in addition to supportive environments needed to focus on learning. As a Special Education Teacher of Students with Multiple Disabilities, I feel they have been the most affected group. For students with special needs, one of the best learning strategies is having a structured routine. The pandemic has stripped this away from them and now parents are left to trying to figure out what works best for their child with the assistance of the teacher. Parents now play a vital role as the co-teacher assisting their child in their daily instruction. Which has left many stressed and overwhelmed with the many changes. The pandemic has had some positive effects as well. It's allowed me as an educator to expand my knowledge of the various online platforms and virtual resources so that I am effective when having to create modified lessons for the multiple levels within my classroom. I've been allowed to be creative to ensure the learning environment is close to or mimics what it would look like if we were in person. My goal is to continue to provide equity and quality resources for my diverse learners.

- **Cassandra Carson**

Teaching during the pandemic has been a challenging experience. The impact on the education experience for children has highlighted the inequities of our society to the residents across the state and country. This was heavily covered by the news at the beginning of the pandemic when the entire state was doing remote learning. As I would watch stories of the digital divide between the high socioeconomic communities and low socioeconomic communities, I was able to directly relate to the latter with my students. There have been great strides to get technology and internet access to our students and this has had a positive impact on learning. Unfortunately, many students do not have the support at home to assist them with the technology and staying engaged with lessons. Online platforms have limitations. No matter how much time is put into novel flashy online classrooms and lessons, the novelty quickly wears off without any necessary benefit. Students need face to face contact with staff and peers for the best educational and social development opportunities, but until the pandemic is under control this is not an ethical reality for the students, staff, or the communities we serve. For the now, we need to do our best to meaningfully utilize our instructional and preparation time efficiently with substance and not bling.

-Tonya Ingram

I feel the pandemic has greatly impacted education for all students especially students with disabilities. Education has shifted tremendously since the onset of the pandemic. Students are now forced to adapt to the new norms of education by doing so virtually with limited resources, support, and understanding. Almost a year later and the transition has not gotten any better. There are constant changes in how to educate students virtually but none of these suggestions take into account how to support students with disabilities. The students I serve are mostly nonverbal and unable to express how this change affects them mentally, socially, or academically. The assessments that are normally in place to gauge the level of mastery has been skewed due to the lack of proximity to students, and the undoubtful support of parents providing the correct and sometimes incorrect responses needed to move students forward or having the information needed to implement an effective intervention plan. Many parents are unable to provide the support a Paraprofessional would normally give in the classroom which greatly limits students' abilities. Being able to meet individual students' needs is trying especially with the students I serve as a lot of their home struggles impact their academic needs. The safe and positive space that is usually created in the classroom, the environment that is designed to block out the ills of poverty, is no longer possible to do virtual learning. But not all aspects of virtual learning are "lost." Virtual learning has uncovered strengths in our students such as computer literacy, virtual stamina (being able to sit in front of the computer for long periods of time), and perseverance (regardless of their struggles many get up each day to do it again). The home to school connection has also increased with many parents being active in students' learning. As an educator, I will continue to deliver the best virtual environment possible for students to achieve at the highest levels, by creating materials to support learning, making learning meaningful and relevant, and providing an equitable and accessible curriculum for all students.

-Pamela Hunter

Since early March 2020, parents, students, and teachers have been burdened with the task of adapting to an online learning environment seemingly overnight. Teachers had to replace physical copies of worksheets with google documents and that isn't always the easiest transition especially for students who might not have internet access at home. In addition, it takes a lot longer to deliver the curriculum and it's been especially challenging to keep students motivated because of all the tech difficulties that the teacher and students face. With that being said, online teaching has forced me to utilize technology in new ways, and I will continue to use many of the skills and applications that I am using to teach online.

-Rhonda Gordon

The pandemic has not only adversely affected teaching, learning, and students, but also the parents of the students. In my experience as a teacher in general, a good relationship between parents and the teachers is crucial. This pandemic has put so much pressure on the parents that they can often be indisposed and may be unable to form relationships or work with the teacher. Sometimes they don't know how, sometimes they are just physically tired, from dealing with so much fallout from the pandemic, that they physically cannot come into video chat rooms with the teacher. This indirectly has adverse effects on the students, and their motivation. Many students are extrinsically motivated; they are only doing work so they are not in trouble with their parents. If you take that motivation away, a lot of students will be reluctant to do anything they don't want to do as a result.

- Mitchell Sommers

The pandemic showed just how big the educational gap is from a social-economic perspective. Parents in urban districts can't afford what suburban communities consider necessities. Absolutely! Scholars and teachers are overwhelmed, not enough focus on social, emotional health for either. The pandemic has impacted education by making it more difficult to access and receive accurate students' accurate grades. Student interaction has decreased tremendously, making it difficult for social-emotional learning.

-Heidi Cruz

Chapter 12: Creating Calm

By Erin Jones
Educational Consultant

On March 9th, 2020, my assistant received a cancellation for a big keynote I was supposed to deliver at a conference in DC. The panic in response to COVID 19 had just begun. I had been hearing rumors of the turmoil the virus was creating overseas. We had not yet understood the implications of a nursing home breakout right here in our home state of Washington. Within the next four days, my entire calendar would be scrubbed as the threat of a pandemic loomed large.

As a consultant, an empty calendar is a REALLY BAD deal. I am no longer on salary with a school district or for the state. When I do not consult or speak, I do not make money. I am the big money-maker in our house. My husband, who is a teacher, makes a regular teacher salary, and his healthcare is amazing, so we benefit there, but the realization that my consulting salary had disappeared overnight was a shock to my system. I will never forget my husband's first words to me as I informed him the evening of Thursday, March 12th, about my professional situation. "Honey, the big bills have already been paid - tuition for Malachi, our cars, the house note. We won't be going out to eat or to the movies anytime soon, but we are going to be fine." Little did we know everything in our state was about to be shut down just days later. There would be no eating out or movies for a very long time. Still, the relief of hearing from "the money guy" in our house that we were going to be fine took such an incredible weight off my shoulders. His calm gave me the ability to get creative. Most important lesson from the pandemic: calm allows for creativity. The opposite - stress, anxiety - prevents creativity.

Education (teachers, administrators, law makers, even students) do not make good decisions or do their best work in moments of stress and panic. This should not be news. We educators know intellectually that stress shuts down parts of the brain.

We have been taught this in a variety of ways during our teacher education programs and trainings on mental health. However, the pandemic demonstrated very quickly that we do not always apply what we have been taught. As the pandemic forced school closures and then a statewide shut-down, I recognized the impact of stress first on decision-makers. I watched the first school district in my state attempt to go immediately online without proper consultation of constituents and state lawmakers. First, there were threats of lawsuits from special education families and then a full-fledged assault that made clear to every other district - DO NOT DO THIS. In that same stretch of a week, I made the decision to provide free Facebook LIVE offerings to children and adults, to offer my online community an alternative to binge-watching Netflix as school districts were trying to figure out how to move forward. I could see the panic in the social media posts of every parent and educator in my feed.

At the time, we did not know how the virus spread, so folks were worried about whether it was safe to go outside, to go to the store. People were locked down in their homes, unsure about how to move forward. My gut instinct was to provide something that would be both a distraction from the fear of the unknown and a learning opportunity. I began to offer a daily read-aloud for small children (two days in English, two days in Spanish, and Fridays in French or Dutch). Over the last three years, I had developed coursework on racial equity for educators. I had at least twenty hours of content that could be spread out over a few weeks. As a former middle and high school teacher who continues to serve as a leader for our church's youth group, I also have an incredible love for 10–18-year-olds, so I decided I should also offer a course based on my TEDx, "Passion for Change", which I decided to call "Becoming a Change-Agent." Friday of that first week, two things happened - a college student sent me a message on Facebook to ask if I had heard of a thing called Zoom. Apparently, his professor used the platform occasionally for class, "that way you could see your students, and they could see you and each other." A Zoom? What was that? I had never heard of Zoom before (I have now spent hundreds of hours on Zoom). That same day, as I came to bed, exhausted from writing lesson plans into the night and then teaching most of the day (something I had not done for years), my husband said, "Honey. I think you're working too hard. You're writing lessons for your teen students, but you have so many friends doing amazing things all over the world. Why don't you just invite your change-agent friends into your classroom and let them tell their own stories?" Why had I not thought of that? Stress. I was just like the district decision-makers who moved so quickly to solve a problem that they didn't consider how their decision might affect others and, therefore, didn't come up with the best ideas. What they attempted to do to help actually caused harm. I had moved so quickly to serve; I hadn't considered what was already in my hand - my amazing friends. I was adding to my own personal stress when there was no need. There were so many people out in my virtual world whose work had also disappeared, who were now stuck at home, eager for something to do, eager to help the world in any way possible.

From March 23 to June 30, my students would learn from (and interrogate) Supreme Court justices, former NFL players, semi-professional athletes, recording artists, authors, spoken word artists and local elected officials. My young students learned quickly that their voices mattered, that adults would actually listen to them. My students learned to speak up and communicate about their needs, desires and passions. They learned from one another to ask thoughtful, provocative questions. My students were so engaged that when their schools were released for summer in the middle of June, they continued to show up in my Zoom classroom. As the days turned into weeks and the weeks turned into months and the months...well, we are getting close to a year of virtual school in my state...I have watched state leaders and district leaders and building leaders and classroom teachers and students buckle under the weight of stress and strain. We have not only witnessed the ravages of a health pandemic. We have witnessed intense racial and political division. We have witnessed the deaths of unarmed Black people at the hands of police and then months of #BlackLivesMatter protests, followed by one of the most contentious Presidential races in modern history. We have witnessed an attempted coup of our national government and then the inauguration of a new President and our first Black and female Vice President. People have lost members of their family and close friends to COVID 19 and cancer and heart attacks and suicide (we have lost nine people in our personal circle). Parents and loved ones have lost work. People of all ages are being affected by the inability to spend time in the presence of friends and loved ones. There are not the same opportunities to express and receive affection. There are also not the same opportunities to navigate and debrief current events in-person, so many have gone on-line to engage in dialogue on Facebook or Twitter, only to discover that conversations on social media in the midst of a health and social pandemic do not inspire or encourage but often add to the already-present stress and strain.

As I speak with students from upper elementary to high school, they are all expressing anxiety about the pressure they are under to perform, to continue to maintain good grades, even when so many are now responsible for siblings and additional chores at home, when they cannot remember the last time they saw their best friend in person. My virtual classroom and other out-of-school convening are the places they get to "just be". It is hard to listen to the pain they express as they talk about their typical school experiences, and it is also beautiful to see the art and poetry and podcasts and TikTok videos they are creating in response to the conversations we are having in our spaces, where we are intentional about practicing gratitude and emotional/mental well-being. Every Monday evening, some friends and I host a gathering of educators and high school students. It is a space in which we practice gratitude and grounding in. We allow each member of the community to show up as they are. We model vulnerability and a brave space, where each member of the community is able to share thoughts about their personal lives or work through a problem of practice from their educational environment. As a community, we have cried with those who have lost loved ones. We have connected others to counseling opportunities. We have helped educators discover tools and lesson plans to effectively address current events. We have brainstormed recommendations for state agencies who have asked for feedback from the public on issues ranging from implementation of Ethnic Studies statewide to whether or not our state should continue grade-level testing. Last week in an interview, someone asked me what I would have done differently had I been elected State Superintendent of Schools. I am very aware of the gift that is my existence outside the system. The culture of American public education is one that is inherently "tyranny of the urgent". Having worked in state government for 4 years and then school district administration for another 5 years, I witnessed leaders doing far too much in reaction to events or complaints or mistakes, instead of being moved by long-term vision for the future, in particular a future that allowed students furthest from educational justice to flourish. I would love to think my ideas for a "better future" would have been inspirational and life-giving, I acknowledge I am not under the same inherent strain and pressure as any of those who are in elected office or who answer to a school board. I have the gift of being unencumbered, of being able to sit in the calm that is outside the system and get creative. What if instead of trying to get things done quickly, we were to focus on engaging more voices at the table, particularly voices who are not usually invited to the table - in particular, students, families? What if more teachers and para educators were invited to the table to talk about what they think would be in the best interests of the system? What if we were to dream a system that created more calm and not as much stress? What if we were to test and grade less and embrace and encourage curiosity and creativity more - both for adults and young people? What if we were to leverage each of our relationships with AMAZING people (young people, adults) and create online content that could be made available across the nation to engage students in creative ways using the technology about which we have now become expert - Instagram, TikTok, Twitter, Zoom, Google Meets? Why couldn't an author like Jason Reynolds do a read-aloud for students across the nation...or Isabel Wilkerson for education staff? If I have learned one thing about education in the last year, it is that we need more creativity and less regulation, more curiosity and less boundaries, more compassion and less judgment. I have witnessed leaders who are given a wide berth embrace new relationships and engage new partners in really exciting work. I have witnessed young people who appeared shy and insecure within the confines of classrooms and crowded buildings step into their brilliance on a Zoom screen. I have witnessed individuals on a screen become community and family, who continue to return to the screen two and three and four times a week to reconnect, to reflect, to energize, even after hours of Zoom classes in a day. If we do nothing else in the next year, may we do all we can to create the calm embrace required for education to become its most curious and creative self. This is what I wish for US post-COVID 19.

Chapter 13: What Matters Most

By E.B. McCall
Gifted Teacher

My elementary students and I had just enjoyed a field trip to the local college where we had explored the science behind sound waves, painted canvases with oils and acrylics, made beaded bracelets using Morse code, folded beautiful origami, created Lego animated movies using green screens, learned to solve Rubik's cubes, made "Bristle Bots" from toothbrushes, and used our wits to solve riddles and secret messages in Escape Rooms. It had been a glorious day filled with learning, laughter, and a lightness that comes from seeing the world through children's eyes full of curious wonder and delight. We had had plans to expand on what we learned on our field trip the following week, but there was to be no follow up. Due to the Covid-19 global pandemic, school was cancelled, and this field trip was our last day together in 2020.

Amidst the disbelief and anxiety of what was happening in our world, I found myself thrust into a new role as an educator. I went from teaching gifted and ESOL (English for Speakers of Other Languages) students in a resource classroom in a small rural school in Southeast Georgia to trying to teach them online, a format with which I was not comfortable nor competent. My immediate concerns revolved around making sure my students were being fed and understood what was going on. The language barrier for my ESOL families proved to be a hurdle, as they did not understand the many messages coming from the school district. They had many questions and called me daily for clarification. Filled with questions like: "How can we get the food being passed out if we don't have a car to drive to the school?; When will the students return to school?; When will the students take the Georgia Milestones Test?; Are the students being held back a grade?; What will happen to the students who do not have computers and internet access? Will they fail?; How do I teach my child to read when I cannot read English?" and more. I served as a liaison between the home and school, as best as I could. I began delivering meals, books, and school supplies to these families who asked for help.

For those families who had computers and internet access, these were trying days, as well. Many families were sharing one computer between several children and parents now working from home. Parents were not anymore familiar with Google Classroom and live meets than the teachers. I had one parent cry on the phone with me, pleading for the online schooling to stop because she was feeling so overwhelmed with it all. Her husband had had back surgery prior to the outbreak, and she was trying to nurse him back to health, work from home, and be a home-schooling mom, all at the same time. I did not know what advice to give her other than to tell her to do what she could, give herself some grace, and not to worry about my class.

Our superintendent aptly said of this time that we were "building a plane while in flight." The situation was very fluid, constantly changing, and stressful. I was receiving mixed messages from my principal and central office administrators. For example, I was being told by one administrator to reach out to my ESOL families and help them, while my principal chastised me for "potentially exposing these families to the Coronavirus." The only thing I wasn't confused about was how confused I was! It was at this point that I realized that I had to take my own advice and do what I could with what I had and give myself some grace. I decided to see this as an opportunity for growth and shift to a focus on what is really important. I continued to check in with my students and their families often. I immersed myself in learning more about virtual learning and digital platforms. I also made a "Flat Teacher Project" and delivered it to all of my students. I gave them a cardstock Bitmoji of myself, similar to that of Flat Stanley, and asked them to take photos and videos of what they were doing with the flat version of myself in the photo too. This was a huge success! Students sent me pictures and videos of them fishing, canning green beans, making felt flowers, reading, writing in their journals, vacuuming, playing with their gecko, cooking eggs, and simply hanging out in quarantine. This project kept the lines of communication open and kept those relationships going, even when we could not be together in person.

Come August, we returned to in-person school. Some students stayed home and continued virtual learning. Most came back to the brick-and-mortar school. We had a "new normal" at school, to which the students and teachers adjusted to easily and flawlessly. Wearing masks, hand sanitation, incessant classroom cleaning, no sharing of school supplies, opening windows to let in fresh air, and social distancing became part of our routine. In between these rituals, we have made other adjustments; those that may serve us well into the future when the global pandemic is gone. We have learned humanity and the importance of social interaction. We have learned to work together for the greater good. We have learned to be resilient and ask ourselves, "What can we learn from this?" We have learned to stop all the busyness and focus on the most important aspects of life.

Having taught 26 years interacting with students

daily, sharing hugs and inside jokes, playing learning games and taking dance breaks, discovering and exploring together, sharing lives and "I love you's," I can truly say that I have been blessed with the greatest profession. I get to know my students and their families on a personal level. We are a part of each other's lives, living in the same community. I have even taught the children of former students. Developing relationships is as much a part of my teaching as developing the mind. When the pandemic took this daily interaction away, being a teacher just wasn't the same. Even now, the students who remain at home, schooling virtually, the closeness just isn't there. The students at home are not interacting with their teachers and classmates in the same way as those at school, and it is my opinion that the social interactions taking place in person are more valuable than those happening online. We are social creatures and we need social interaction and human contact.

To make this in-person schooling happen to create these social interactions, we have to work together for the greater good. We have to all wear our masks, clean our hands, stay home when exposed to sickness and follow the mitigation guidelines. We must be flexible and help out where needed. Since we are short on substitutes when teachers are out, I've filled in in other classrooms, served breakfast, and packed lunches for children to take home. I've worked with my ESOL families to help secure internet service for them by filling out paperwork for free and low-cost internet assistance. I've delivered half-finished projects and books we are reading to student homes, when they were quarantined. My students have learned how interconnected the world is; that we are battling the same virus and experiencing many of the same struggles. It has been the year of flexibility and patience with one another; the year of compassion for our fellow man. We are at our best when doing for others and this pandemic has taught us how important that is.

Through this time of extraordinary change, we've learned to be adaptive, innovative, and resilient. How we operate school is different. Students play outside in different areas of the campus. Students skip a seat at lunch or eat in their classrooms. There are no visitors on campus, no field trips, no "Fall Flings," no holiday parties, no faculty meetings, and no co-mingling of classes. We have taken virtual field trips and adapted holiday activities to make them safe for students. We've learned how to hold team meetings spread out while wearing masks or to meet virtually through Microsoft Teams. We've incorporated Google Classroom into our daily routine, so that if and when students must quarantine, they can keep up their studies when at home. We've secured laptops and internet access for those in need, making online education accessible and equitable for all. We wrote grants to have school lunches paid for all students, regardless of income. We've taken online teacher trainings and courses to help us better meet the needs of our students in the digital age. This pandemic has been a testament to just how resilient we are as educators to be flexible and creative problem solvers in the face of adversity. This global pandemic also forced us to stop, ever so abruptly, with the busyness of life and focus on what is really important. In education, standardized test scores were found to be not as important in a global pandemic as making sure students were fed, safe, and happy. Teacher effectiveness ratings were found to be less important than making teachers feel supported and encouraged. Awards presentations, class parties, field trips, and growth percentiles were now not as important as building relationships with each other and keeping each other healthy. The pandemic was a gift; a shift in perspective to focus on what matters most: humanity, benevolence, teamwork, compassion, love, and relationships.

Chapter 14: Work with The Willing

By Jeff Mather
Artist in Residence

A rtists and educators often move in different spheres, only crossing paths when there's a connection made through a family member or mutual friend. Both groups do work that demands creativity but there may not always be immediate rapport between them. An innovative arts organization in Macon, Georgia called, The Art Factory, brought Atlanta artist, Jeff Mather, to work with the fifth-grade students and teachers at Monte Sano Elementary in Macon many years ago. Mather is a community-based public artist and teaching artist, and he was asked to coach this team at Monte Sano to collaboratively design and fabricate a new public art project for Pendleton King Park, about 1/2 mile from the school. One of the fifth-grade teachers at Monte Sano at that time was André Mountain.

Though he was an artist himself, performing intermittently in the local spoken word scene, he expressed later that he wasn't sure that having his fifth-grade students working on an ambitious large scale environmental sculpture was the best use of their limited time in a school day. He wanted them to excel academically, and time spent making art seemed, at first, like time being subtracted from their academics. But Mather and Mountain struck up a friendship during this arts infusion partnership anyway and they stayed in touch over the years, even during the years that Mountain was working in the Pacific Northwest. Since Mountain's return to Georgia, he and Mather's paths have crossed at the STEM/STEAM Forums that the Georgia Department of Education convenes, and Mather has begun serving as the design coach for the Urban Agriculture program that Mountain has initiated at Marbut Elementary. Mather has been the STEAM Artist-in-Residence for 45 days each semester at Drew Charter School in Atlanta, since 2012, increasingly embracing the burgeoning STEAM ed and Maker ed movements and co-teaching with Drew teachers in all subject areas and all grade levels and Mountain has increasingly embraced the power of arts infusion as key to transforming and bringing greater equity to education.

"Work with the willing!", the storyteller said to me. I always listen to the storyteller. He has been a friend and a colleague for many years. Knowing as many stories as he does, he is often able to listen to my sputtering about my struggles and quickly cut to the chase. He can pare my circuitous pondering down to what is essential.

We met because we are both well established in a field that many people aren't aware exists, the teaching artist field. This is a professional field with its own professional journal and international conferences and yet a lot of artists don't even know that channels exist for serving communities this way and earning a living this way. We have had organizations in Georgia come and go that connect teaching artists with schools. State agencies, county school system programs, state chapters of national arts organizations such as Young Audiences and VSA

Arts, have carved pathways for educators to locate and begin working with teaching artists of all kinds, in a wide range of art forms and from a variety of cultural backgrounds. Some of us have even helped to build and run arts infusion non-profit organizations and crafted mission statements with language that we hoped would lead to deeper partnerships between educators and artists. We have become grant writers and developed relationships with foundations in our efforts to keep these organizations going. Funding for the arts can be, too often, a political football and I suspect that the people who are sitting in positions where decisions about arts funding get made may have grown up in families that didn't make a point of going to art museums or plays or concerts. So they may be uncertain about how vital the arts are in our communities.

The COVID-19 virus pandemic threw so many curve balls at people in every walk of life. There have been tragic consequences for many families and the normal rhythms of home life and work life have been thrown out of whack. For independent contractors, who work with schools, like teaching artists, having school buildings closed down has presented layers of challenges. Though my own partnerships have been primarily with STEAM educators and have included projects with teachers in Robotics, Spanish, Music, Physics, Math, Engineering, Dance, and Digital Media, my main art form is sculpture. I'm a community-based public artist and environmental sculptor and I'm best known for coaching large scale collaborative outdoor site sculpture projects. As it began to really sink in for my educator partners, as adapting to the pandemic restrictions began to shake up how everyone was going to need to teach, with learning going online, they asked me, "So how are you going to keep on doing what you do? You focus on collaboration skills and hands-on tool use. Can you still be our artist-in-residence on Zoom?"

Being endlessly flexible and adaptable is key to working in schools. Even in a regular school year the ground often shifts beneath your feet. You may show up on any given day ready to run workshops and discover that everyone you thought you'd be working with is heading down to the auditorium for an assembly program or getting on buses for a field trip that hadn't been on the calendar. As a visiting artist you just have to roll with a level of unpredictability and not let this inherent uncertainty rock your boat too much.

I have enjoyed having so many artists as friends and colleagues and I've found myself jumping into co-residencies with many of these wonderful people when opportunities to do that have come along. I know the way I approach being a teaching artist based in visual arts has been changed for the better because of all that I've learned from dance artists and music artists and theater artists. I'm certain that I've especially benefitted from gaining understanding from these performing artists about collaboration and improvisation. One of the first agreements in improv is to have a "Yes, and" stance. This means finding a way to contribute something to a collective effort without negating anyone else's offering. I now see that my coaching of 3D design is a "Yes, and" approach. This kind of an approach to art making is one of the reasons that students who teachers perceive as disengaged seem to pivot unexpectedly when working with a teaching artist and exhibit real engagement, I think. I've become accustomed to the students I work with being truly engaged. They are excited to be learning how to use power tools and handle expensive materials and they get a taste of the power of art making when their projects permanently change the school environment. That is what I'm used to seeing anyway. A spirited exchange of ideas during the collaborative design process, "yes, and", followed by skills acquisition when they learn what their bodies can do as they make big art together, their faces shining seeing their accomplishments appreciated by their community.

And now, for months, I see those faces in Zoom rectangles looking sleepy, looking disengaged, looking glum. Dispirited. My STEAM partner teachers text me before the classes that they have asked me to co-teach are about to start and say, "We can't just keep talking to them! We've got to get them doing something! Making something! What can you get them to make?" The school has provided every student with a bag of materials but none of the stuff in the bag is for 3D design work. I scramble. What can you make when you don't have materials? I look around my own kitchen and spot the recycling basket with a stack of glossy junk mail in it. I figure everybody gets junk mail, so I start improvising a way to make tabletop architectural models out of junk mail. By the time the Zoom class is beginning I've got a 10-inch-tall model of a sculptural information kiosk that can have science data visualization graphics projected inside of it to show them. The glue is still drying. Man, this is winging it! But I'm in the struggle with these students. We are going to do something. We are going to make something. Soon, odd junk mail structures are being held up to their laptop cameras and I express enthusiasm for their efforts, their experimental spirit, and I see a smile or two. They are willing to try new things.

Damn the torpedoes, the setbacks, the strangeness of only seeing everyone online. We can still find that spark that the arts provide us. I've watched my friend the choreographer run dance workshops on Zoom, and she makes it work. Her natural charisma still comes through and she has learned to interact with students in their little rectangles and connect with them and get them moving. My friend the textile artist has gotten excited about using conductive thread and LED lights, venturing into new territory making digital quilts. And she's not waiting until she is physically back in school buildings to share this new way of making art with students. She wears a different colorful hat every day and easily gets and holds the attention of these online learners. The storyteller is finding new audiences for his stories. He has been asked by the Kennedy Center in Washington D.C. to make a series of short videos of his stories and they are distributing these to schools across the country. Necessity does breed invention and innovation.

Because the pandemic has restricted our ability to travel, I have shifted into new ways of doing what I do, too. This "great pause", as some have called it, has opened up more space for thinking about how our work as teaching artists serves as a catalyst for learning across the curriculum and how the arts offer real tools for addressing larger issues in the world. I've found myself in the thick of multiple, overlapping, collaborative projects with other teaching artists during these last several months that have had me delving into how arts-based activism can contend with systemic racism and climate change and disability rights and urban agriculture more deeply than I might have otherwise. I have become involved in forming international partnerships with educators and scientists and other teaching artists and will be traveling to do this work post-pandemic. I see no shortage of willing partners to do these dances with and we will have stories to tell.

Chapter 15: Leading with Love

By Juawn Jackson
Bibb County School Board Member

As I finalized my decision to run for the Board of Education a few weeks into 2020, my vision focused on three main issues: 1) how to best support students, educators, and parents, 2) how to realize our shared desire to educate students, and 3) how to prepare them for a 21st century global environment. However, as March 2020 made its debut, we found facing a once in a generation challenge: battling a highly contagious virus in the third quarter of a school year. I must admit, I never thought I would begin my term of service in the middle of a global crisis, but then again, who could? Unfortunately, our national political climate on the national level has further complicated our recovery efforts and prolonged our ability to safely begin what has become our new normal. As I began the Spring as a newly sworn in board member, I looked forward to beginning this phase by doing what I have always done: serving my community. I planned to greet students as they arrived at school, coordinate advocacy development forums for parents, and yes, even help to serve lunch in the cafeteria. I ran a campaign focused on fiscal responsibility, attracting new businesses to our community, and safer schools. COVID-19 continues to challenge each of these goals and make its presence known.

A major theme of my campaign was leading with love. Our students, parents, and educators must know that their leaders genuinely care about them. During this pandemic, care must be shown through grace and understanding. For students, that grace is shown through the prioritization of their mental health and providing them with as many wraparound services as possible. Students do not need an excessive number of assignments spread across numerous platforms during this pandemic. Rather, we should provide them with a minimum number of assignments per subject area that shows their mastery of the content standards. Additionally, many of our students already faced challenges of learning loss in a typical summer, but now they also have to navigate the magnitude of additional loss due to COVID-19.

Leading with love also extends to our parents and families. We must make sure that they know that we truly want them to be our partners in education and not just observers. Quite honestly, we need them because we cannot do this work alone. It will take all of us working together with innovative and open minds about how and when we educate our students. I remember reading an article in the New York Times about a public charter school in Newark, New Jersey that is offering kindergarten and first grade classes in the evenings to better assist working parents and students that need more hands-on assistance. Now is the time to reimagine how we facilitate learning by partnering with parents to usher in limitless growth in our students' performance.

Leading with love and understanding also requires a listening ear, starting with listening to our educators directly. Platforms that allow teachers to speak directly with their Superintendent and Board members should not have the impression of sidestepping school leadership, but rather to provide an unfiltered analysis and understanding of the climate with those on the frontlines. Any opportunity to offer layers of protection in the classroom and our school buildings should be strongly considered and implemented before returning educators to their physical classrooms with students. I was proud that my district took steps to safeguard the air quality in our schools by installing bipolar ionization devices, designed to eliminate infectious pathogens and purify the air. Our educators should certainly be comforted by the fact that his school district will not put them in unsafe environments, even as the pandemic continues.

Lastly, leading with love requires making sure all of our students' needs are met. This pandemic has clearly highlighted the importance of wraparound services. As a candidate for the Board of Education, I spoke about these services often. It is difficult to learn when your stomach in growling. It can be hard to keep a focused mind when you are worried about where you will lay your head at night. I believe that we can truly change the trajectory of a generation through our investment in these services.

COVID-19 has exposed countless vulnerabilities within our educational system, but also reaffirmed the need for ethical, competent, and transformational leaders on every level of the spectrum. I still believe that people value the truth and appreciate decisions based on science and data. We all are anxious to being our new normal, but during these times I am constantly reminded of Rev. Dr. Martin Luther King Jr.'s warning to us, "We must learn to live together as brothers or perish together as fools." Wearing a mask, socially distancing, washing hands, etc., should have never been used as tools of political divisiveness. The road to our new normal has been prolonged because of this issue, and the wellbeing and educational advancement of our students have been undeserving casualties. As an African American male, educated in public schools and raised in public housing, I am deeply concerned with the correlation of COVID-19 and the achievement gap.

McKinney & Company estimates that the projected learning loss due to this pandemic could set African American students back ten months as opposed to six months among White students, and nine months among Hispanic students. Again, it is going to take transformational leaders who are willing to facilitate conversations that lead to new initiatives that reimagine education to fill these gaps and set our students on the trajectory toward a more equitable future.

The actions we take, the conversations we have and the matters we focus on for the next several months will have major implications for a generation of American school children. I remain optimistic that that we will come out of this pandemic stronger than ever, with our heads held high, ready to educate and ready to learn from the experience of finding our way forward after having been virtually lost.

CONTRIBUTORS

Dr. Marchell Boston

Educator | Author

Dr. Marchell " Marc" Boston is an award-winning educator, who currently serves as the principal in the DeKalb County School District (metro Atlanta). He is a "turnaround" principal, who has 22 years of school-based leadership. He has served as an elementary school teacher, a school counselor, as well as an assistant principal. Dr. Boston has worked in higher education for 16 years, serving as an adjunct professor at Strayer University, Capella University, and Thomas University. He is a proud alumnus of Morgan State University, where he earned a B.S. in Elementary Education. He has advanced degrees from Fort Valley State, Jacksonville State and Argosy University. A native of Atlanta, Ga, Dr. Boston currently resides in metro Atlanta with his family. He currently authoring, Finding Freedom: A Principal's Journey.

•

Jonie Lao Harris

Educator

Jonie Harris is a child of immigrants who escaped genocide in Cambodia. She overcame many barriers growing up, one of which was learning English. Determined at a young age to be successful, she is a first-generation college graduate and is on the pathway of pursuing her National Board Certification. She has been in the education field for 17 years and is currently a 3rd-grade teacher in one of the most diverse schools in the country. She has been recognized by Tacoma Public Schools for her powerful individualized small group instruction. She regularly serves as a mentor for teachers and shares her expertise in teaching with colleagues in meetings and Professional Development seminars. She has been acknowledged consecutively for student growth, strong classroom management, and maintaining a highly engaged classroom. She is passionate about pushing her students to their fullest potential by having high expectations and holding them accountable for their actions.

Juawn A. Jackson

School Board Member

une 2020, Juawn A. Jackson was elected as the youngest member to the Bibb County
ard of Education. Professionally, Mr. Jackson serves as a Project Advisor for Alpha Phi Alpha
ucational Talent Search. Mr. Jackson graduated from Mercer University with his master's
gree in Higher Education Leadership in May of 2018. He received his undergraduate degree
m Georgia College & State University in Political Science and earned a certification in
adership.

Erin Jones

Education and Systems Consultant, Coach, Public Speaker

Erin Jones has been involved in and around schools for the past 26 years. She has taught in a variety of environments, and in some of the most diverse communities in the nation. Erin received an award as the Most Innovative Foreign Language Teacher in 2007, while working at Stewart Middle School in Tacoma and was the Washington State Milken Educator of the Year in 2008 while teaching at Rogers High School in Spokane. She received recognition at the White House in March of 2013 as a "Champion of Change" and was Washington State PTA's "Outstanding Educator" in 2015. After serving as a classroom teacher and instructional coach, Erin worked as an executive for two State Superintendents. Erin left the Office of Superintendent of Public Instruction 5 years ago to work in college-access at the school district level. She left her job to run as a candidate for State Superintendent and was the first Black woman to run for any state office in Washington state, a race she lost by a mere 1%. She is a nationally-recognized educator (20+ yrs), consultant, and public speaker.

Baruti Kafele

Leadership Expert | Speaker | Author

One of the most sought-after school leadership experts and education presenters in America, Principal Kafele is impacting America's schools! He has delivered over two thousand conference and program keynotes, professional development workshops, parenting seminars, and student assemblies over his 34 years of public speaking. Principal Kafele brings a reflective approach to delivering his message. It forces his audiences to look deeply within themselves toward assessing their own practices to a level of "discomfort within their comfort." His reflective approach creates a basis for transformative change and improvement.

Jeff Mather

Artist in Residence | Site Artist

Jeff is a community-based public artist and multi-disciplinary teaching artist. He has conducted site sculpture residencies and directed public art projects all over Georgia. He is board president of the Atlanta Partnership for Arts in Learning (APAL). He is the STEAM Artist-in-Residence at Drew Charter School for 45 days each semester, where he co-teaches project-based learning units in K-12. His partnership work at Drew has been featured by GPB and Edutopia and has received two Innovations awards from the Governor's Office of Student Achievement. Jeff was digital storytelling coach for nine years at the South Atlanta School of Law and Social Justice and he has created digital storytelling programs for the Woodruff Art Center, for APAL, and at Drew Charter. He has directed experimental theater productions at the Center for Puppetry Arts and served as artist-in-residence for the Atlanta Symphony and the High Museum. Jeff has served as a artist-in-residence at over 150 schools.

E.B. McCall

Gifted Educator

EB McCall is a 28-year veteran teacher for Wayne County Schools, in Southeast Georgia. She has taught all grades Pre-K - 12th and presently teaches elementary gifted and ESOL (English for Speakers of Other Languages). McCall has been honored as Coca-Cola's and Walmart's Teacher of the Year. She earned her M.Ed. from Georgia Southern University and six-year degree from Nova Southeastern University. She is currently working on her doctorate in Curriculum Studies from GSU. McCall has a passion for developing student leaders, giving students a voice and choice in their learning, and being an advocate for her students and their families.

William Mustafa, Jr

Videographer/Photographer
and International Content Creator

William Mustafa, Jr. is an award-winning videographer/photographer and International content creator, currently working on location in Italy finalizing his upcoming monograph, "Lost in Translation". He is the official photojournalist for the US Kickboxing Olympic Team and will be participating in the upcoming World Games in the United States in 2022.

Ms. Iantha Ussin

Educator | Author

Ms. Iantha Ussin, MAT, is a highly qualified, veteran middle grades English Language Arts teacher. When she's not in her classroom, she offers her expertise in P.O.W.E.R Teaching and classroom management to teacher candidates and new teachers in colleges and school districts across the country through keynote addresses, professional development sessions, workshops and guest lectures. Ms. Ussin is the author of "Your Classroom or Their Playground" (May 2021 release), a deep dive into what teachers should and should not do in a classroom that is expected to be continually conducive for learning.

André Benito Mountain

ANDRÉ BENITO MOUNTAIN

EDUCATOR | AUTHOR | SPEAKER

www.andrebenitomountain.com
defeducation@icloud.com
IG @andrebenitomountain
Facebook @andrebenitomountain

WHO AM I

André Benito Mountain is an educational advocate, school principal, and a relentless champion for new approaches to be integrated into today's ever-changing academic environment. He is a regular contributor to Education Post, Education Week, Citizen Ed and Principal Magazine. He is the author of "Principals Don't Walk on Water", "The Brilliance Beneath", and "The Mountain Principles". He is the creator of "Taking Notes: Jazz and the American Story", an interactive presentation designed to increase student engagement in African-American history that combines storytelling, Jazz music, and lessons from America's past through the lens of Jazz. He and his daughter are the founders of Def-ED Clothing, an apparel line inspired by urban culture and designed for educators.

André is an advocate for innovations in curriculum/instruction development, and technology integration . André's belief in high expectations from educators, students, and administrators inspires others to explore arts-infused teaching strategies to connect with students. He inspires a new generation of teachers to leverage their creativity to change the lives of children. André Benito Mountain is a visionary educator who lives by his creed: *Stay positive. Work hard. Make it happen.*

CORE VALUES:

Leadership | Social Justice | Cultural Responsiveness | Teacher Autonomy | Authenticity | Courage | Service

INTERESTS:

Arts Integration |Equity, Transformational Leadership | Concurrent Learning | Virtual Learning | Restorative Practices | Chess in Schools

SPEAKING TOPICS:

Arts Integration in Schools | Jazz and American History | Hip-Hop History | Hip Hop as Literature | Chess Programs in Schools | Writing Across the Curriculum | Transformative Leadership | Urban Agriculture in Schools

WWW.ANDREBENITOMOUNTAIN.COM

BOOKINGS: CONTACT MS. BROWN AT (470) 238-9903
OR EMAIL DEFEDUCATION@ICLOUD.COM

Made in the USA
Monee, IL
19 April 2021